IMPROVING
READING, WRITING, AND CONTENT LEARNING FOR STUDENTS IN GRADES 4-12

IMPROVING

READING, WRITING, AND CONTENT LEARNING FOR STUDENTS IN GRADES 4-12

ROSEMARYE T. TAYLOR

CORWIN PRESS
A SAGE Publications Company
Thousand Oaks, California

For information:

Corwin Press
A Sage Publications Company
2455 Teller Road
Thousand Oaks, California 91320
www.corwinpress.com

Sage Publications Ltd.
1 Oliver's Yard
55 City Road
London EC1Y 1SP
United Kingdom

Sage Publications India Pvt. Ltd.
B-42 Panchsheel Enclave
Post Box 4109
New Delhi 110 017 India

Printed in the United States of America

Library of Congress Cataloging-in-Publication Data

Taylor, Rosemarye, 1950-
Improving reading, writing, and content learning for students in grades 4-12 / Rosemarye T. Taylor.
    p. cm.
Includes bibliographical references and index.
ISBN 1-4129-4226-8 or 9-7814-1294-2263 (cloth) — ISBN 1-4129-4227-6 or 9-7814-1294-2270 (pbk.)
    1. Language arts (Elementary)—United States. 2. Language arts (Secondary)—United States. I. Title.
LB1576.T354 2007
428.4´071—dc22

                                        2006014231

This book is printed on acid-free paper.

06   07   08   09   10   10   9   8   7   6   5   4   3   2   1

Acquisitions Editor:	Elizabeth Brenkus
Editorial Assistant:	Desirée Enayati
Production Editor:	Jenn Reese
Copy Editor:	Cheryl Rivard
Typesetter:	C&M Digitals (P) Ltd.
Proofreader:	Caryne Brown
Indexer:	Nara Wood
Cover Designer:	Audrey Snodgrass

Contents

List of Figures

Preface

As I look back on my professional journey, it is easy to see that literacy has always been the first and foremost purpose of my work. As a naive first-year teacher, I was thrust into an environment in urban Atlanta where my sixth-grade reading and language-arts students read between first- and third-grade levels. This was my introduction to below-grade-level readers and the lifelong quest to find solutions. From that time forward, my number one focus has been to research, design, implement, and evaluate strategies and systems to improve reading, writing, and hence content learning. Although my work has been grounded in research, it is confirmed in action research in diverse schools with a wide range of teachers and students.

As you consider the ideas and suggestions within this text, keep in mind that about 55% of elementary students read on grade level, about 45% of middle school students read on grade level, and only about 35% of high school students read on grade level. Much of this can be attributed to the differences in the expectations of the assessments from elementary to middle to high school, which are related to the amount of nonfiction (science and social studies) reading and levels of questions on the middle and high school assessments. This trend in reading scores will be addressed and corrected only with consistent implementation of research-based instructional strategies in all classes in all grade levels. In a recent meeting of executive administrators in a diverse district of 80,000 students, the executive director for high schools attributed the gains in the district's high school reading to the consultation and support provided by the concepts and strategies in this book. I hope that readers will find success with the practical suggestions within.

Acknowledgments

Antoinette (Toni) Worsham, supervisor of English/language arts/ reading and foreign language in the Mobile County Public School System in Alabama, had encouraged me for years to write a teachers' book on developing readers, writers, and content learners in Grades 4 and up. Toni's leadership in a very diverse and challenging district is a model for pushing the higher achievers even higher and pulling up everyone else! Thank you, Toni, for being a role model and for your encouragement.

There are many others to be acknowledged who have assisted teachers in improving literacy across schools in kindergarten through twelfth grade. These exemplars have implemented consistency in reading, writing, and content learning across grades and academic areas. Listed here are those who invited me into their schools and districts, and from whom I gratefully borrowed examples of excellence included herein.

Brennan Asplen and faculty, Millennium Middle School, Sanford, FL

Darvin Boothe and faculty, Lake Brantley High School, Altamonte Springs, FL

Frank Casillo and faculty, Lyman High School, Longwood, FL

Nancy Fuleihan, reading specialist, Southwest Middle School, Orlando, FL

Debbie Graves, principal of alternative schools, Orlando, FL

Carlotta Iglesias, former principal, Stonewall Jackson Middle School, Orlando, FL

Althea Jackson, Lillian Gividen, and faculty, Hiawassee Elementary School, Orlando, FL

Peggy Jones and faculty, Sebastian River High School, Indian River, FL

Marshall Kemp, administrators, and faculty, Logan County Schools, Russellville, KY

Deborah Peterson, visiting teacher/school social worker, Cobb County Schools, Marietta, GA

Shaune Storch and faculty, Lake Howell High School, Winter Park, FL

Bill Vogel, administrators, and faculty, Seminole County Schools, Sanford, FL

John Wright and faculty, Timber Creek High School, Orlando, FL

Corwin Press gratefully acknowledges the contributions of the following individuals:

Christene Alfonsi, Teacher
Fairfield Senior High School
Fairfield, OH

Allyson Burnett, Instructional Interventionist
Alief Hastings High School
Houston, TX

Janet Hurt, Associate Superintendent
Logan County Schools
Russellville, KY

Raymond Lowery, Associate Principal of Instruction
Alief Hastings High School
Houston, TX

Martha Jan Mickler, Independent Literacy Consultant
Strategic Literacy Consulting
Bellair Beach, FL

Cathy Puett Miller, Independent Literacy Consultant
Huntsville, AL

About the Author

Rosemarye (Rose) T. Taylor has a rich background that includes beginning her career as a middle and high school reading, language arts, and Spanish teacher. She also has served as a middle and high school administrator and as a district-level administrator in Georgia and Florida. In private-sector management, she was Director of Professional Development for Scholastic, Inc., New York. Currently, she is Associate Professor of Educational Leadership at the University of Central Florida in Orlando.

Much of her success is due to conceptualizing, creating, and implementing fail-safe systems that work seamlessly to support improvements in student learning. As an example, Rose led the research, design, and implementation of the Orange County Literacy Program, which has successfully impacted thousands of elementary, middle, and high school students and teachers. The classroom concept designed with her leadership has been produced as a literacy intervention product by Scholastic, Inc. In Orange County Public Schools, Orlando, Florida, she designed and implemented a curriculum system including curriculum, instruction, assessment, and staff development supporting the notion that systems make the work of administrators and teachers easier. Through working to support the development and implementation of learning communities to advance student achievement, principals have the structure within that empowers the classroom teachers to make gains day by day.

At the University of Central Florida, her specialty is instructional leadership. She has conducted research on leadership particularly as it relates to accountability. Presentations on this topic have been given at the University Council of Educational Administration, American Association of Educational Research, American Association of School Administrators, International Reading Association, Association for Supervision and

Curriculum Development, National Association of Secondary School Principals, and National Middle School Association conferences. Her articles have been published in journals such as the *Phi Delta Kappan, Educational Leadership, Middle School Journal, Schools in the Middle, American Secondary Education, AASA Professor, The National Staff Development Journal, Principal Leadership, The School Administrator,* and *International Journal of Education Management.* Four books, *Literacy Coaching: A Handbook for School Leaders, The K–12 Literacy Leadership Fieldbook, Literacy Leadership for Grades 5–12,* and *Leading With Character to Improve Student Achievement,* reflect the commitment to all students learning more through leadership that creates ethical fail-safe systems, particularly literacy systems. She serves as a consultant to schools, districts, and professional organizations, such as Phi Delta Kappa and ASCD, in the areas of literacy, creating district and school literacy systems, small learning communities, curriculum system development, and leadership.

The Fail-Safe Classroom

Improving Reading, Writing, and Content Learning

INTRODUCTION

With release of The National Reading Panel Report (National Institute of Child Health and Human Development [NICHD], 2000) and the response from the No Child Left Behind Act of 2001 (NCLB), there has been a renewed focus on literacy learning initially in the primary grades and more recently in Grades 4 through 12. In the primary grades, students are learning to read. In contrast, in Grades 4 through 12, students are expected to read to learn content, and yet there are students who still need to learn to read *and* to read their content texts to access the standards-based curriculum. Many teachers from Grades 4 through 12 are frustrated in their teaching of mathematics, science, social studies, health, technology, and electives since the students have difficulty reading the textbooks, which are often written above grade level. A fourth-grade teacher recently shared with me that she conducted a readability test on the fourth-grade social studies book and found that it was at the tenth-grade level. No wonder the students have such a difficult time!

This issue continues in middle school and high school, where independence in accessing content text is expected to a greater degree. Providing support to address this concern, Biancarosa and Snow (2004) identified a critical element of effective adolescent literacy programs as "effective instructional principles embedded in content, including language arts teachers using content-area texts and content-area teachers providing instruction and practice in reading and writing skills specific to their subject area" (p. 4). The emphasis on improving reading, writing, and content learning in Grades 4 through 12 and teachers' needs for a doable systematic approach—regardless of grade or subject matter taught—are the focus of this text.

Although some of the examples and strategies found in the text may stretch some paradigms, they are based in research and proven in practice working with teachers in diverse schools. As a result of using the ideas, teachers and students experienced more success on a daily basis, and school data reflect higher student achievement overall.

As an educational community, we have worked toward but not achieved the goal of NCLB of all children reading on grade level by the end of Grade 3, but we are slowly making progress. The Nation's Report Card (www.nationsreportcard.gov) identifies results of the 2005 National Assessment of Educational Progress (NAEP) for both fourth and eighth grades. From 1992 to 2005, nationally the percentage of fourth graders on or above *Basic* did not change significantly, but the percentage performing on or above *Proficient* increased. For eighth graders, there was an increase in the percentage on or above *Basic* and no significant change in the percentage scoring at or above *Proficient*. Exacerbating the lack of significant gain is that from 2003 to 2005, eighth-grade students lost 2 points! The good news is that the average score for White, Black, and Hispanic students increased and the achievement gap between White, Black, and Hispanic students decreased, although during the time period measured numbers of Hispanic students increased. These NAEP data support the sense of urgency for all classrooms in Grades 4 through 12 to support both literacy learning and content learning as much as possible.

There are many excellent teachers who accomplish this expectation every day, and for them, this text should confirm their good work. For others, this text seeks to provide support and guidance and to be a source of reflection for continuous improvement. To begin the journey of creating and reinforcing classrooms that improve reading, writing, and content learning, let's first reflect on excellent classrooms that we have known. These are classrooms where all students seem to thrive. These classrooms are fail-safe: Teachers create the environment and instructional experience for all students to maximize literacy learning and standards-based achievement.

Close your eyes and visualize (use all the senses—see, hear, feel, smell, touch) one of those classrooms.

What did you see in the classroom?

What were students doing?

What did you hear?

How was the classroom organized?

Where was the teacher, and what was the teacher doing?

The one I visualize is a seventh-grade social studies class where students are reading and writing while learning about world cultures—improving all three at the same time.

There are students all around the room, seemingly doing different things. A few are at their desks writing, trying to resolve something in the text that is puzzling them. Others are using the Internet to research the perceptions of their peers in other countries. Two are in the back of the room practicing a PowerPoint presentation, The Middle-Level Years in Three Different Cultures, which will be shown on the school's closed-circuit television system during the daily announcements. Three just came back into the classroom after reading to younger students the book they had written and illustrated, *Tamales on Christmas.* Five are sitting at a trapezoid table with the teacher, conferencing about their writing and receiving feedback from one another. Students seem happy, even joyful, although their work is at a high level. These students work hard, feel valued, and develop intellectually and socially in a safe, supportive environment where they use the literacy processes and strategies to achieve high levels of thinking.

Jotting down your answers to the questions posed above will help you formalize your ideas of a fail-safe classroom for literacy and content learning. Before the optimally successful classroom for literacy and content learning is developed, we must know what it is and what it is not.

ACADEMICALLY AND PSYCHOLOGICALLY SAFE TO LEARN

Fail-safe classrooms for literacy development and content learning are academically and psychologically safe. This means that they are supportive of all students working on standards-based meaningful and challenging work; that is, they have equal access to rigor.

Most teachers will describe their classrooms as safe and supportive. Think beyond traditional conceptions of physical safety to "safety to learn." Safe for each student means that each one has equal access to the standards-based curriculum through incorporation of literacy processes and research-based literacy strategies and experiences of the classroom. To achieve such safety, each student must be met where he or she is in the learning continuum (Tomlinson & Kalbfleisch, 1998) and provided the appropriate support, processes, and instructional resources to grow. Learning is differentiated, with some students getting different kinds of instruction and different instructional resources. This aspect comes from the teacher considering three elements that are essential for creating the community of learners, a condition of the fail-safe classroom. These essential elements are the classroom community, the student, and the text resources.

Classroom Community

Basically, the classroom community is developed through consistent student-centered decisions on the part of the teacher. Eric Jensen (1998) suggests that such classrooms are absent of emotional threat, value relationship building, and have frequent feedback, clear goals, and choices for students. This classroom community makes it psychologically safe to learn. Students do not have the fear of put-downs or being laughed at by either other students or adults in the room. Incorrect answers are seen to be opportunities to think, to clarify, and to support a response rather than a negative response like, "NO!" Teachers who create a community of learners first attend to developing the classroom community and getting to know the students. After those relationships have begun development, the teacher will turn his or her attention to the text to be studied.

Classroom community motivates by including clear goals and by providing reasonable choice for students in assignments and choice in showing how much they have learned. Other evidence of a classroom community is the literacy-rich, print-rich classroom. While some think of print rich as being purchased resources, classroom libraries, and professionally developed print, it also means the display of student work. When a classroom is a community of learners, it is student owned. I can walk into the classroom and immediately know what is being studied by the evidence of student literacy and content learning, displays of student work, and student products.

Student

By the time students reach upper elementary, middle, or high school they display many different levels in their academic and literacy backgrounds. They have learned or not learned many different vocabularies, concepts, and skills. This is why building common background knowledge for all students is important. Those who know less are well aware of their deficiencies and often feel neither emotionally nor academically safe unless the teacher infuses literacy strategies to scaffold students to success (Graves & Fitzgerald, 2002). Creating success through careful scaffolding develops students' personal motivation to achieve.

Each student's culture and economic status impact background knowledge, vocabulary learning, and life experiences that either accelerate or make difficult comprehension. This is why building background knowledge and explicit vocabulary instruction are essential (Irvin, 1998). Some classrooms embrace only certain cultures and economic backgrounds, but those that are academically and psychologically safe respect and consider as strength the diversity within a learning environment. Creating a safe, supportive environment means that every student feels significant and respected as an individual making progress toward competency as a learner.

Text Resources

Think of the worst teacher you have ever known and picture or visualize (using all your senses) this person in your head. Where did this teacher begin on the first day of school each year, with the classroom community, the student, or the text? You are correct; the worst teachers begin by immediately assigning reading in the text in the name of rigor! In my experience observing teachers for more than 30 years, I have seen that these teachers have lower student achievement and less rigorous evidence of learning than the teachers who begin by getting to know the students and their academic backgrounds and by building the classroom community. As the teacher gets to know the students' backgrounds related to the standards-based content to be learned, he or she will be more strategic in developing appropriate instructional experiences for the students.

When we think about text considerations, we first think about the structure of the text. Good teachers in all grade levels and in all content areas begin with strategically teaching students how to read the text, where to find important information, and how to learn without reading word for word. It is an erroneous assumption that even good students understand text organization as the teacher does. For example, teach the students to read headings, boldfaced words, and sidebars. Essential information is generally found in these areas. Teach students to preview the text before attempting to read the paragraphs. Previewing means to read the titles, headings, and sidebars. It also means to read the pictures, diagrams, maps, charts, and graphs (multiple-symbol systems).

Figure 1.1   Community of Learners

Classroom Community	Student	Text
Academic and psychological safety	Background knowledge Vocabulary	Structure
Motivation: Choice, clear goals	Literacy strategies	Vocabulary
Literacy rich Print rich	Personal motivation	Respectful and relevant
Student owned	Culture and economic status	Accessible rigor

Understanding strategies used by each text for introducing vocabulary and assisting with its acquisition are critical to providing access to the content. Each publisher may use a different technique for introducing vocabulary. Most will have key vocabulary highlighted or boldfaced. This helps little in science, where a chapter may have as many as 30 new vocabulary words!

Well-selected texts have relevancy to and respectfulness of students. Historically, many texts have had biases and underrepresented many of our students. Publishers are savvy to the changing student populations, so providing students with respectful, relevant instructional resources is a fairly easy task, but one to be strategically addressed.

Teachers who improve literacy learning provide relevant, respectful texts supplementary to the core text in the content area. Newer editions of literature anthologies, science, and social studies texts have companion texts and support materials for those students who read below grade level. These texts have explicit strategy support for comprehending the rigorous on-grade-level content standards. Providing access to the rigors of a standards-based curriculum begins with creating a community of learners.

NONNEGOTIABLE EXPECTATIONS OF DAILY PRACTICE

Along with creating a community of learners, the fail-safe classrooms incorporate nonnegotiable expectations of daily practice to ensure equal access to both literacy development and content learning. Teachers who are consistent with the expectations of daily practice have positive changes in student achievement regardless of the grade or subject taught.

Figure 1.2   Nonnegotiable Expectations of Daily Practice

- Classroom is print and literacy rich.
- Teacher uses the processes of literacy: reading, writing, speaking, listening, viewing, thinking, and communicating with multiple symbol systems.
- Teacher reads to and with students on-grade-level texts.
- Teacher teaches, models, and practices strategies of expert readers and writers with students.
- Students read independently with accountability.

SOURCES: Taylor & Collins, 2003; Taylor & Gunter, 2005.

Nonnegotiable 1: Literacy-Rich and Print-Rich Classrooms

In the description of the academically and psychologically safe classroom, the first nonnegotiable was mentioned: All classrooms are literacy and print rich, at all grade levels, even for seniors! As we move up the grades from elementary to middle years to high school, the concept of literacy and print rich tends to diminish. This lack of literacy- and print-rich materials is consistent with the lower student literacy achievement documented as it declines from elementary to middle school to high school. Literacy and print rich means the classroom reflects the student learning at that time. It is not a bulletin board welcoming students back from their summer break with changes in athletic schedules as the seasons change. Nor is it the elementary classroom with only teacher-made displays of seasons and academic concepts to be studied. In contrast, at all levels the bulletin boards and academic displays are probably student developed or are displays of student work. In other words, these classrooms are print rich—not decorated. For teachers who use more authentic assessment and less pencil-and-paper tests, creating a literacy-rich environment will be natural.

Print rich also means that each classroom has a classroom library reflecting the content learned in the classroom and the reading levels of the students. Ideally, the percentage of books that are nonfiction will reflect the expectation of the standardized assessment: about 50% at the elementary level, about 60% at the middle level, and 70% at the high school level. Excellent nonfiction and informational text can be located on your librarian's professional resource Web sites, state resources like www.Sunlink.com, and publisher Web sites such as www.Scholastic.com.

If you are wondering how you will accomplish obtaining a classroom library, there are several ideas that work. The first is to go to the principal and ask for a budget to order a classroom library. You will need to have an amount in mind, and perhaps even an order list to substantiate your request. Books vary in cost, from the *Blueford Series* at $1.00 each to those beautiful collector books that may cost $50.00 each. Think about checking out of the school or public library the expensive books, and focus the purchase request on inexpensive paperback books.

You may also consider having a class book club or schoolwide book fair. Depending on the amount of orders, free books are earned from the vendor. A parent or community volunteer may be available to coordinate the orders and the book fair event.

Don't forget to advertise to students, parents, and community groups that you are soliciting books for the classroom. Be sure to review any books donated for appropriateness. You can always trade inappropriate books for appropriate ones at a used-book store.

Nonnegotiable 2: Using the Processes of Literacy

Literacy processes are reading, writing, speaking, listening, viewing, thinking, and communicating through multiple-symbol systems that develop simultaneously as a student's language grows. These processes are used to learn the vocabulary, content, concepts, and skills of all content areas studied. For this reason, developing all of the literacy processes in every content classroom is critical for every student. Often, by the time students reach fourth grade, they struggle with the difficult vocabulary, fluency, and comprehension necessary for reading the content text without extensive teacher assistance. The instructor who assigns reading of the on-grade-level textbook and does not incorporate the other processes will make less progress in literacy and content learning than the one who develops them all simultaneously.

Listening is not passive. Listening means that students are making meaning by organizing their thoughts, drawing relationships between what is being read to them or what they hear and what they already know, and drawing conclusions. They may be completing a graphic organizer to keep track of their thoughts. While students are listening, the teacher is pausing, probing, asking questions, and encouraging predictions and higher levels of thinking. While students are listening, they are developing their speaking skills and background for reading and writing.

Articulating clearly, organizing thoughts, and communicating orally are essential to developing excellent readers, writers, and content learners who can communicate what they are learning. In fail-safe classrooms, teachers use formal English and academic language of the content area they teach. This means they use exacting terms and do not dumb down or baby the content by using less than formal terms. The practice of using casual rather than formal academic content language insults the students' abilities to grow in vocabulary and language usage. For students to use accurate academic content language in their speaking and writing, they must hear it in multiple venues and multiple times (NICHD, 2000). Although it may not be the norm, students should be encouraged to use formal English, academic language, and accurate content vocabulary while speaking in complete sentences at all times.

Reading, writing, and listening develop speaking skills. This will surprise those who work hard at keeping the students from talking! In fact, if you provide purposeful opportunities to speak, expect appropriate academic language, and provide feedback, you may find that extraneous unrelated talk diminishes. Practicing speaking in front of the class or to a peer about what is being read is critical. A quick strategy is to ask the students to turn to their partners and explain the concept just discussed for two minutes. Or, turn to your neighbor and ask the questions for which you need answers to understand the chapter; take three minutes to do so. Speaking and using academic language in a more sophisticated way helps to develop reading and writing skills and vice versa.

What is viewing? Viewing means looking, seeing, and taking in clues that provide meaning. This meaning is called a mental model, visual, or, in some cases, anchored instruction (Cognition and Technology Group at Vanderbilt, 1990). Those teachers who gain the most learning from their students will open a unit with visuals, short vignettes or video clips, streaming video on the Internet, demonstrations, or models. These upfront experiences with concepts and vocabulary provide students a mental model on which to "anchor" their new learning. This experience provides students who may have had interrupted schooling or for whom English is their second language the background knowledge that is essential for learning the new content concepts and language.

Viewing has a particular meaning related to the use of multimedia, which is ever present in our lives and the lives of our students. Burmark (2004) reported that we process visual information about 60,000 times as rapidly as text and that such viewing can improve learning up to 400 percent. We want students to develop their expertise in viewing, to understand and to be discriminating in what they view—on television, the Internet, CDs, visual and performing arts, and in print. Viewing supports students in developing content knowledge but requires the development of the other literacy processes. A previously mentioned example is previewing the text or conducting a picture/visual walk-through of a text chapter prior to reading the text. This walk-through develops vocabulary, concept, and content knowledge and prepares the student for reading the text.

In our technological world, students need to view expertly. To do this, a student must be able to read, to write, to speak, to listen, and to think. The literacy processes are interdependent in their use and development. Viewing is a critical literacy process that will continue to gain in importance as our reliance on technology increases.

Communicating with multiple-symbol systems is always present in schools. Multiple-symbol systems include symbolic representations that are found in each content area. Examples include the periodic table, mathematical symbols, scientific notation, technology, art, music, movement, maps, graphs, and charts. You may think of some other multiple-symbol systems. Being an expert reader and writer requires the reading, speaking, and writing about these various multiple-symbol systems. Reading comprehension assessments include passages with charts, graphs, maps, and other symbol systems and are often labeled the research and reference strand. These naturally appear in content texts. Skill with comprehending these symbol systems and expressing the comprehension in writing is essential to improving achievement on formalized assessments.

Readers are probably surprised to see that we list thinking as a literacy process. Can you read without thinking? Can you write without thinking? To make meaning, to translate ideas into print, a student has to think. Thinking is implicit in literacy development. Comprehension is thinking. Keeping thinking in the forefront of our literacy processes also ensures that we will provide students with meaningful work. Such work communicates that we believe they can think, and it requires them to think. Thinking connects directly with the higher levels of analysis, synthesis, and evaluation, which we will delve into in Chapter 6. Students demonstrate operating at these high levels through other literacy processes. Thinking at a high level is possible for every student, even very young ones, and encourages the development of content knowledge, skills, and concepts, as well as language, vocabulary, and comprehension.

Developing all of the literacy processes simultaneously will impact learning. Greatest improvement will take place with deliberate and purposeful incorporation of reading, writing, speaking, listening, viewing, thinking, and communicating with multiple-symbol systems into instructional plans.

Nonnegotiable 3: Reading To and With

The third nonnegotiable is for teachers to read to students and with students every day using on-grade-level standards-based content. A student can comprehend about two grade levels higher than his independent reading level when hearing the pronunciation and having eyes on print. The higher oral language comprehension is why teachers are encouraged to briefly model how fluent readers read a textbook, a piece of nonfiction, or fiction with students every day. It is not entertainment but the opportunity to teach the vocabulary and essential content concepts. Since this is instructive, it is not round-robin reading but reading by a fluent reader—probably the teacher. It may also be an audiotape, DVD, or CD that accompanies the textbook or other shared text.

Reading to and with students also supports developing lifelong readers (Trelease, 2001). Hearing a fluent reader read with expression and comprehension develops the joy that motivates students to want to read more and to reread the shared reading text. In addition to Trelease's well-known *The Read Aloud Handbook* (2001), readers may want to access *Read-Aloud Anthology* (Allen & Daley, 2004), which includes a variety of selections for upper elementary through high school. Reading to and with naturally leads to independent reading, the next nonnegotiable.

Nonnegotiable 4: Teach, Model, and Practice Strategies of Expert Readers and Writers

When teachers read to and with students, they are teaching, modeling, and practicing the strategies of expert readers and writers, showing that reading has meaning and is joyful. On-grade-level readers have developed their own strategies for comprehension if they have not been taught specific ones. Below-grade-level readers do not understand that good readers are strategic and that they too can become strategic and develop greater comprehension. Below-grade-level readers are not the only ones who benefit from explicit comprehension strategy instruction; on-grade-level readers who have difficulty with specific types of text, like science or technical reading, improve comprehension with strategies. Direct, explicit instruction in comprehension strategies is recommended in *Reading Next: A Vision for Action and Research in Middle and High School Literacy* (Biancarosa & Snow, 2004). Research-based comprehension strategies are delved into more deeply in Chapter 5.

Nonnegotiable 5: Accountable Independent Reading

The fifth nonnegotiable expectation of daily practice is that students read independently every day on their reading level and teachers hold them accountable for doing so. The suggested amount of time is 20–30 minutes each day. It is important that the independent reading is a book, because the teacher and student can match the book to the student's independent reading level. A student can easily be held accountable for completion of the book and for upward growth into higher-reading-level books. More important, as surprising as it may seem, many struggling students reach twelfth grade and admit they have never read a book until they find this just-right book and get hooked on reading. Therefore the student selects the book he or she will read on his reading level that is of personal interest.

Daily accountability means that the student probably maintains a reading log of the dates of the reading, last page read, and a short summary, or connection to the current day's reading, or prediction about the next day's reading. When teachers ask students to read a certain number of pages or note the number of pages read, it becomes inefficient if the students cannot find the page to begin reading the next day, and it does not support comprehension improvement.

After reading the entire book, an overall accountability that gives the student choice and the opportunity to demonstrate joy in the reading is important. Giving a book talk or making a storyboard or poster of the book is a good way for students beginning in Grade 4 to show with joy that they have read a book. An example of a visual that a ninth-grade teacher displayed in her room uses the traditional graphic of introduction, rising action, climax, and falling action. The students write on the graphic the associated events in their independent reading book. Accountable independent reading is revisited in Chapter 4, "Developing Fluency in Reading All Texts."

NONNEGOTIABLE EXPECTATIONS OF DAILY PRACTICE AND WRITING

These nonnegotiable expectations of the daily practice of reading to students, reading with students, and students reading by themselves apply to all classrooms. After students have read or been read to, they write. In all grade levels, students write about what they heard or read, what it meant to them, how it relates to something else they have read, or how it relates to their world. Teachers who are making progress do not teach or assign writing out of the context of reading. Vocabulary and language of the lessons are modeled and taught through the reading and are expected in the writing. The more students read, the better their writing and comprehension will be. They just can't help it! These nonnegotiable expectations of daily practice will be addressed throughout this book with practical applications. Consistency in application of the concepts of fail-safe literacy classrooms—community of learners and nonnegotiable expectations of daily practice—will ensure improvement in reading, writing, and content learning.

Mental Model: Fail-Safe Classroom for Improving Reading, Writing, and Content Learning

Here is an example of an English-as-a-second-language classroom I was in at Lake Brantley High School in Altamonte Springs, Florida. What took place in this classroom could have taken place in any classroom at any grade level. Mrs. Gutierrez created a close-knit community of learners from a number of cultures in the Caribbean, South America, Asia, and Europe. As you enter her room, on the right she had beautiful displays of interesting books. At the end of the display and book case is a listening center; in December when I was there, *Great Expectations* was the audiobook in the center. Farther down the right wall was a bulletin board, labeled Wonderful Writers, full of student writing. At the right angle of this wall and the end of the room were computer stations for student practice and writing. The front of the room was covered by a whiteboard, on which was written vocabulary words that were reviewed prior to listening to an audiotape and following along with the text to *A Christmas Carol*. An audio player was there as well. The left side of the entrance to the room housed resources on bookshelves. Where were the students? In the center of the room, tables were placed together so that 4 to 6 students worked in a group.

Bordering the top of the four classroom walls was the word wall. Students created the word wall as they discovered words they did not know and brought them to the attention of the class. As a student introduced a word to the class with discussion and understanding following, the student owning the word completed a 5 × 8 card with the word, definition, and nonlinguistic representation of the word. Then the word was added to the word wall, creating a functional classroom resource for all students and documenting their growth as proficient English-language learners.

The instructional experience of the day focused on *A Christmas Carol*. After introduction of the new words, the students found their places in the text. As the students listened to and followed along with the chapter, when they came to one of the new vocabulary words, Mrs. Gutierrez stopped the audio player and discussed the use of the words *in context*. Following the "reading with" instructional experience, the students worked in groups on comprehension responses to the reading. This classroom is literacy and print rich, building on the strong community of learners, the uniqueness of the students, and the text being studied. It also includes the nonnegotiable expectations of daily practice.

Creating the Fail-Safe Classroom for Literacy and Content Learning

Beginning the journey with visualizing a classroom that works helps you to think about what you already have in place and what you may select as your entry point. Many teachers begin with creating a literacy- and print-rich environment by visiting with their media specialist and checking out a relevant collection to keep in their classrooms for a period of time. Reflecting on your own practice and thinking about how you may celebrate the exemplary instruction that you have and how to add more exemplary instruction will inform learning as you read Chapters 2–6.

Finally, to create a fail-safe literacy system for the classroom, the family and community must substantively engage in the learning process, and in Chapter 7, we look at proven ways to make this a reality. Now, glance over the practical tips that follow, then turn the page and consider the role of literacy components in Grades 4–12.

PRACTICAL TIPS FOR CREATING FAIL-SAFE CLASSROOMS FOR LITERACY AND CONTENT LEARNING

To review and engage thinking, specific instructional strategies that support both literacy learning and content learning are offered. They reflect the academically and psychologically safe classroom and the nonnegotiable expectations of daily practice. One might think that instructional strategies should vary from fourth grade through twelfth, but in practice there is such a diversity of literacy development and content learning across these grades that explicit instruction and scaffolding are recommended for all grade levels. The first ones are important for all classrooms and all teachers of Grades 4–12. The second group targets content classrooms beyond language arts specifically.

Tips for Grades 4–12 Reading, Language Arts, and Content Areas

- Be explicit and clear about directions and expectations. Provide them in print, not just orally.
- Give one set of directions at a time. Let students complete that task, then give the next set of directions. Multiple sets of directions confuse even the most accomplished students and overwhelm others. Scaffold the students to success.
- Teachers of grade levels, academies, integrated teams, or houses create a plan to ensure implementation and assessment of accountable independent reading. Reading Counts or Accelerated Reader may play a part in the accountability.

- Teach students the structure and features of the textbook. Students should know to read headings, look for boldfaced words, and read sidebars. Where does the author place important information? Where is the information you think is important?

Tips for Grades 4–12 Content Areas

- Introduce new information, concepts, and so on with visuals, discussion, introducing essential vocabulary, and accessing and building on prior knowledge before asking students to read and do book work. Remember that many students will not have the prior knowledge expected by the publisher, so think of your role not as accessing prior knowledge but as providing it.
- Create print-rich classrooms appropriate for your content area:
  1. Create bulletin boards or word walls with vocabulary, definitions, and visuals. (Have students do this!)
  2. Check out book collections from the library related to your content curriculum. Be sure to cover the range of readers and interests. Include audio books or CDs that support the content.
  3. Post student work related to the curriculum.
  4. Create time lines, maps of events, literature, and so on. (Students should do this also!)
  5. When you show videos, use the English captions.

- Consider alternatives to the quizzes for lower readers. It is always best to provide choice in how students demonstrate comprehension. Choice is a motivator.
- Be sure that all print placed in front of students is in the format they are expected to use in their own writing. Using formats for writing other than those used in language arts or English or on state assessments creates a confused mental model. Block formats are commonly used in worksheets and lessons printed from the Internet. Remember the power of viewing, and consistently place accurate mental models in front of students.
- Preview the text to be read with the students, focusing on headings, sidebars, and titles. Previewing should also

(Continued)

(Continued)

include graphics, pictures, maps, charts, and diagrams (multiple-symbol systems).

- Ask students to write a 1-sentence summary for each visual in the chapter before you assign the reading of the text.
- Divide the class into teams of 3 or 4 students and ask each team to explain a specific picture, visual, graph, chart, or map.
- Ask students to write a short explanation of problems after they are solved.

Reading Components in Grades 4–12

Creating a community of learners and using the nonnegotiables of daily practice will assist the teacher in developing a classroom poised for improving reading, writing, and content learning regardless of grade or content area responsibility. Implementation of the nonnegotiable expectations includes infusion of the five essential components of effective reading instruction identified by the National Reading Panel Report (NICHD, 2000). In this chapter, they will be introduced, particularly as they relate to students in Grades 4–12. These five components of effective reading instruction are (1) phonemic awareness, (2) phonics, (3) vocabulary, (4) fluency, and (5) comprehension. In this chapter, the main focus is on phonemic awareness and phonics. Vocabulary, fluency, and comprehension are discussed in more depth in Chapters 3–5.

Have you ever listened to a student struggle to read orally out of a mathematics, science, or social studies textbook? This struggle may indicate a lack of phonological awareness and fluency and is common throughout upper elementary, middle, and high schools. For students to be good readers, they must have mastered phonemic awareness and phonics, which generally is expected to have occurred by the end of third grade if not before. They must also have on-grade-level vocabulary, fluency, and comprehension. From third grade on, teachers put most of their energy into vocabulary and comprehension instruction, leaving out phonics, phonemic awareness, and fluency. With greater accountability measures in place in most states, more attention is now being paid to students in Grades 4 and above who have not mastered phonemic awareness and phonics, which is probably about 5% of the student population. In many schools and districts, particularly high-poverty or high-second-language districts, the percentage is much higher.

PHONEMIC AWARENESS

Phonemic awareness refers to the understanding that words are made up of phonemes or parts and that these parts have sounds associated with them when spoken. Keep in mind that oral language development precedes print language development and is related to phonemic awareness. Therefore, with phonemic awareness students are making connections between what they hear and what they say.

Phonemic awareness instruction should start with simple phonemes of identifying a sound. After demonstrated success, the teacher will move to blending phonemes. Students may next identify a word when a phoneme has been deleted or another added or substituted. Scaffolding phonemic awareness instruction in this systematic manner will support students in learning new words. According to *A Closer Look at the Five Essential Components of Effective Reading Instruction* (NCREL, 2004), students who have had systematic phonemic awareness instruction should be able to identify a word in print, its meaning, and its pronunciation, by relating it to already mastered oral language.

Students initially pronounce simple phonemes and eventually should be able to put them together and pronounce more complex words. For instance, at first a student can pronounce *man* and later can put *man* together with other phonemes to pronounce *manipulate* or *maneuver.* As teachers teach phonemes, they should have the words in print so students can associate the sounds with the words and meanings. Students need strong phonemic awareness skills for phonics instruction to be successful. For students to become fluent comprehenders (those who make meaning) of text, pronunciation should be automatic so that their working memory can focus on making meaning.

PHONICS

Phonics means that students understand the symbols of the alphabet and that these symbols have associated sounds when they are in written language. Simply, phonics refers to written language, and phonemic awareness refers to spoken language. When we put the parts of words together, either written or spoken, we have sounds that carry meaning.

Ideally, students reach fourth grade and have mastered these two reading components, but it is not always the case. In addition to the students who struggle with these two components, we also have a steady influx of English-as-a-second-language learners for whom our alphabetic and sound/symbol system may be new. These students need direct instruction on phonics and phonemic awareness regardless of their age or grade, and yet we cannot insult them with the type of instruction that young children in the primary grades receive in their classrooms. In observing afterschool tutoring of Haitian middle school students, it was clear that they were working on phonemic awareness and phonics in English. Findings of the National Reading Panel Report (NICHD, 2000) include that systematic phonics instruction produced substantial improvement in reading and spelling up through sixth grade and especially for special-needs students. Although we typically think of phonics instruction for kindergarten through third grade, we cannot ignore the needs, even if in only a few students, in upper grades.

RELATIONSHIP OF NONNEGOTIABLES TO READING COMPONENTS

When teachers consistently implement the nonnegotiable expectations of daily practice, they are addressing the reading components, particularly vocabulary, fluency, and comprehension. For those students in Grades 4 and up who need support with phonemic awareness and phonics, the teacher will need to go beyond the nonnegotiables as previously described. Figure 2.1, Relationship of Nonnegotiables to Reading Components, is a graphic display of how they relate to the fail-safe literacy system introduced in Chapter 1.

Note that at the bottom of Figure 2.1, two periodic nonnegotiables, word study and test preparation, have been added. Consider these two to be part of a systematic approach to improving student achievement, but they should take place periodically within each month, not on a daily basis. The goal is for students to read on grade level and to be good writers and content learners, not to be good test takers. The research on test taking supports infusing test-taking strategies into instruction, rather than stopping instruction and preparing for test taking (Langer, 2000). The bottom line is good readers do well on standardized assessments.

RELEVANT AND RESPECTFUL LITERACY FOR BELOW-GRADE-LEVEL READERS

Keep in mind that the academically safe classroom will assist in thinking about ways to support pronunciation while respecting the developmental

Figure 2.1   Relationship of Nonnegotiables to Reading Components, Grades 4–12

Nonnegotiables	Reading Components				
Daily	Phonemic Awareness	Phonics	Vocabulary	Fluency	Comprehension
Use processes of literacy: read, write, listen, speak, view, think, express with multiple-symbol system	Practice oral language both heard and spoken related to print	Identify sound/symbol relationships when introducing new words	Introduce vocabulary, concepts, content prior to reading & writing. Use viewing & mss to develop mental models of vocabulary	Develop vocabulary, model fluency. Practice (choral reading, response reading, partner reading)	Enhanced by reading/writing after use of other processes. Use all processes, not read/write only
Read to and with students (on-grade-level, fluent reader, audiobook, CD, teacher)	Model spoken and heard language	Model sound/symbol relationships	Teach in context	Model fluent reading	Provide access, teach strategies, model meaning making
Teach, model, practice literacy strategies			Direct teaching, mapping relationships		Provide student ownership for independent practice
Read independently with accountability (choice, on reading level)			More reading, greater vocabulary, better writing	Reading & rereading build fluency. Tape reading, listen, reread & retape	Practice strategies, accountable for daily connections, visualization, summary, etc.
Print-/literacy-rich environment	Listening centers, technology support	Word walls, concept maps	Visuals of vocabulary, concepts, relationships	Reading the room practices fluency	Makes sense and meaning of words
Periodic Nonnegotiables					
Word study			Creates independent word solvers	Improves rate	Necessary for independent comprehension
Test preparation			Application Practice		Application Practice

stage of the student. Knowing that oral language development precedes print language development is a key factor in determining practice. You may recall that the processes of literacy are reading, writing, speaking, listening, viewing, thinking, and communicating with multiple-symbol systems. By using viewing along with listening and speaking first, students can train their ears in the correct pronunciation of words and begin to understand their meaning by anchoring the concept with viewing, prior to the expectation of independently reading the words in print.

Appropriate pronunciation and oral language practice with print ever present will help make explicit the sound/symbol relationships. When introducing vocabulary to below-grade-level readers, pronounce each word carefully, syllable by syllable, "si-mi-le." Then, ask the students to chorally pronounce the word "si-mi-le." Now, pronounce it individually. The teacher should explain what a simile is, providing examples and nonexamples along with a nonlinguistic representation. Now ask, "Who can tell us what 'simile' means?" "Who can point out an example in the text?" "Who can make up a sentence using another simile?" This example may seem elementary to some readers, but I have observed it working successfully even with urban high school students who were in intensive intervention. Tip: Follow all strategies with comprehension questions to ensure development of understanding and not the development of word callers.

Another example of explicit oral language and print-aligned instruction would be to provide an agenda on the board each day. Read the agenda to the students. Discuss the agenda, and then ask students to read it back to the class as confirmation of the pronunciation and comprehension.

In the print- and literacy-rich classroom, teachers refer to word walls and curriculum maps regularly. Do not just put these resources up as displays, but make them integral parts of the classroom. Regularly ask students to use them, read orally from these instructional supports, and explain them. In addition, ask students to continually add to these curriculum maps and word walls. Students, not the teacher, should own them. Such resources in the classroom should be used before, during, and after reading as well as during writing, continually supporting development of language both heard and spoken, along with reading and writing.

A developmentally appropriate strategy is to incorporate minilessons using poetry, songs, and other rhyming words. Students enjoy these kinds of learning experiences and do not see them as demeaning. Sing the songs that include appropriate content vocabulary to ensure content learning and phonemic awareness. Mathematics and science teachers find success with music that includes difficult concepts.

Continual oral language development is essential for the older students who have not mastered phonemic awareness. Models for oral language development should always be fluent speakers and readers of English. These may be adults, students, or technology solutions. Developing opportunities for speaking about content learning individually, in pairs, or in small groups will be helpful. For example, "Take two minutes and share with your partner what you think is most important related to the passage we have just read," or "Explain to your neighbor how you solved the problem." All responses should be given in complete sentences and should take only a few minutes of class time.

Mental Model: Musical Mathematics Lab

In a low-performing urban elementary school that is working hard to improve achievement, I observed a mathematics lab where fourth- and fifth-grade students performing close to grade level, but not on grade level, were engaged with mathematical music. This music directly gave instruction in on-grade-level mathematical vocabulary and concepts. When the students were given pencil-and-paper tests on the vocabulary and concepts, they performed amazingly well, convincing me that the musical mathematics lab was a success. Further convincing me was that I observed more engagement, confidence, and accuracy with mathematical work in the musical mathematics lab than in the regular classrooms where teachers were instructing on similar concepts. The lab was an excellent support in developing students who were proficient in mathematical language and concepts.

READING INTERVENTION AND PHONEMIC AWARENESS

For direct instruction on phonemic awareness in a reading intervention or English-as-a-second-language classroom, there are some other ideas to consider that are more basic than those previously described. Regardless of the age or grade of the student, if the student needs this type of instruction, then it is appropriate. Provide students a sample word, like "girl." Ask students to write as many words that they can think of with the same beginning sound while you time them for 30 seconds. Next, ask them to write as many words that they can think of that rhyme with "girl" while you time them for 30 seconds. After each of these exercises, ask students to orally share their words and perhaps reward those with the longest correct lists. From these one-syllable words, move to two-, three-, and four-syllable words. You could even have students write as many four- or five-syllable words they can think of. This begins to be challenging, but fun also. Students who are working on this basic level should keep a notebook of Words I Know. By dating each time words are added, they can visually keep track of their increasing list of words they can decode. Create celebrations of milestones like 100 words, 200 words, or even 1,000 new words.

TECHNOLOGY SOLUTIONS

Reading Intervention

When students reach fourth grade or higher and do not have strong decoding skills, then they should be targeted for immediate intensive intervention. This intervention will be most successful if it has a technology component. Biancarosa & Snow (2004) identified a technology component as one of the essential elements in improving literacy learning in middle and high schools. In addition to the research support, another reason I make such a direct statement about the need for a technology component is that otherwise, the student will probably be successful only with one-on-one tutoring, which generally is not as cost-effective as a technology solution. Technology solutions for decoding will first assess the student's ability to decode high-frequency words. Then the software will prescribe learning experiences, specifically taking into account the student's decoding proficiencies. One measure of the software will be the diversity in the prescriptions of learning experiences provided for different students. The individual prescription is the strength of excellent software. In addition to individual prescriptions, look for oral support in pronouncing the words, identifying words, and in spelling words. Students may record words and receive feedback on the correctness of the pronunciation. Examples of software that work well include *Simon Sounds It Out* (Don Johnston Publisher), *Fast Forward* (Scientific Learning), and *Read 180* (Scholastic, Inc.). These technology solutions use strategies that a skillful teacher would do one-on-one but seldom has the time to accomplish. Also, the learning experience may even be provided in a virtual environment appropriate to the student's developmental stage, culture, and experiences.

If you are considering incorporating technology solutions but are not sure how to evaluate the effectiveness of the solution to your students' needs and school environment, ask the vendor to provide research-based support on use of the solution with students similar to your target students in an environment similar to yours. Another idea would be to check with www.metiri.com. This Web site is hosted by an organization, The Metiri Group, that evaluates technology solutions based on what the publisher states the software will accomplish. The evaluations are objective and may be helpful to you in understanding the appropriateness of particular solutions for your targeted needs.

Content Classrooms

In content classrooms, students seldom have the opportunity for targeted technology solutions for the below-grade-level readers. Most

English, language arts, science, and social studies textbooks have audio or compact disc support that accompanies their purchase. Many teachers use these supports as time permits. In contrast, think about using these audio and visual supports consistently with your students to provide modeling prior to reading and during reading of the text. Also, you may have students whom you will allow to take home the audio and visual supports to assist with content learning and phonological awareness development at home.

Setting up a listening station or center with technological resources and texts will be a good idea for creating a classroom that will support developing readers of content texts. Such a listening center may have technology solutions that go along with the textbook and may also have fiction and nonfiction audiobooks that complement the content being learned. Students should maintain a log of what they have read.

When showing instructional videos to support standards-based content curriculum or DVDs, turn on the English closed captions. This will assist students in drawing relationships between the written and spoken words while they see the visuals. A few minutes of a video are sufficient to create a mental model and understanding of concepts. Long videos tend to take more learning time than they are worth, even though students enjoy them.

In addition, encourage below-grade-level readers to turn the English closed caption on when viewing television or DVDs at home. Sound-symbol relationships, vocabulary, fluency, and comprehension will be seamlessly and painlessly improved. This is particularly helpful for English-as-a-second-language students.

Mental Model: Textbook Adoption

One of the large districts that I work with was adopting social studies instructional resources during the 2005–2006 school year. The social studies supervisor and the teacher committee that recommends resource adoption had as one of their priorities to adopt textbooks with audio and technological support as described, because of the emphasis in reading and developing both literacy and content learning in all grades. The large district referenced has a renewed priority of all the subgroups of students in all schools (elementary, middle, and high schools) improving in reading, writing, and content learning.

AUDIOBOOKS

Audiobooks are motivational for students as they model both pronunciation and assisting students with sound-symbol relationships while providing access to quality text. My personal preference is that audiobooks be unabridged. The reason for this is that the unabridged version gives access to high-quality literature and language that serve as a model for students. One of the resources best known for unabridged audiobooks is Recorded Books (www.recordedbooks.com). On the Web site you will find selections by theme, genre, age range, or even by awards. Figure 2.2, Coretta Scott King Award Recorded Books, provides an example of timely motivational books for young readers.

Recorded Books also has SmartReader selections for middle and high school students who read below grade level. These are probably for use in the intensive intervention reading class. These selections come in two reading levels: Grades 1–2 and Grades 3–4. The student can adjust the speed slower if he or she is having difficulty following along or faster once the student is beginning to read more fluently. Although at a lower reading level than the student's grade level, the interest is high, as can be seen from Figure 2.3, Example of SmartReader Selections.

Figure 2.2   Coretta Scott King Award Recorded Books

Title	Author
Fallen Angels	Walter Dean Myers
Day of Tears	Julius Lester
Forged by Fire	Sharon M. Draper
Heaven	Angela Johnson

Figure 2.3   Example of SmartReader Selections

Smart Reader Level	Title	Author
2	*Nowhere to Hide*	Jean Marie Stine
1 2	*Reverend Martin Luther King, Jr.*	Sandra I. Fox Ted Gottfried
1	*The Tell-Tale Heart*	Kallie Wilbourn
1 2	*Twister*	Sandra I. Fox Mark Wise

SOURCE: www.recordedbooks.com

PRACTICAL TIPS FOR PHONICS AND PHONEMIC AWARENESS SUPPORT

Tips for Grades 4–12 Reading, Language Arts, Reading, and Content Areas

- During the first week of school, ask each student to record one paragraph out of his textbook. Listen to the recordings at your leisure, even driving home from school. Quickly and easily you will know who can decode or fluently read the textbook and who cannot. This suggestion was made by a high school science teacher.
- Practice new vocabulary chorally before addressing meaning.
- In whole-class instruction, have fluent readers read out loud, in contrast to nonfluent readers.
- Maximize oral language support, including technology solutions (compact discs, audiobooks, English closed caption when viewing).
- Create a listening center appropriate to the content being learned.

Tips for Reading Intervention and English-as-a-Second-Language Class

- In small groups or individually, work with those who struggle the most.
- In small-group work with the teacher, oral reading by students for practice and coaching is a good idea, particularly in intervention classes.
- Maximize the power of technology solutions. Software targeting phonics and phonemic awareness should be used with older, below-grade-level readers when needed.

Owning Vocabulary 3

Not only do we want students to learn specific vocabulary and academic language needed to comprehend content text, but we also want students to become independent in understanding and owning vocabulary. In this chapter, strategies for accomplishing the vocabulary ownership challenges are offered, keeping in mind that the most assured way for students to own large vocabularies is to read, read, and read some more in a variety of texts and to have direct instruction on academic vocabulary.

When I enter a faculty gathering and ask for those who teach vocabulary to raise their hands, all teachers will have a hand in the air! Teachers raise their hands because every textbook has a list of vocabulary to be learned. It appears that the most common strategy for learning vocabulary is for students to look up the definitions in the glossary or dictionary and write them down. Unfortunately, this is the least effective method for learning vocabulary and can consume 20–30 minutes of class time on a regular basis. Why is looking up definitions and copying them into a notebook an ineffective method? The most obvious reason is that most words have several definitions depending on the context in which they are found. Students tend to write which definition? Right! Students write down either the shortest or the first. In either case, the definitions rarely fit the context of the word used in the text. Second, writing down someone else's definition fails to give the student ownership and understanding of the word.

Simply stated, the most effective way to directly instruct vocabulary is for the teacher to introduce the target words, briefly explain them, and provide a nonlinguistic representation. Nonlinguistic representations can be graphic organizers, models, pictures, drawings, webs, or other nonalphabetic representations. Then the students should provide a definition in their own words and their own nonlinguistic representation (Marzano, Pickering, & Pollock, 2001). The nonlinguistic representations significantly enhance the retention of the vocabulary words. Over time, the words should be used multiple times in multiple ways using all of the processes of literacy.

VOCABULARY SOLVERS

The goal of vocabulary acquisition is not memorization but owning vocabulary strategies so that students can decipher meaning and comprehend text independently. Word study is viable and was introduced as a periodic nonnegotiable in Chapter 2. Word study includes acquiring automaticity (immediate recognition and understanding) with frequently occurring words typically taught in primary grades, such as articles, pronouns, prepositions, verbs, and nouns, and frequently occurring academic vocabulary (Marzano, 2004). Lists of frequently occurring words (found in Marzano, 2004) are thought to be basic to content reading the way multiplication tables are basic to mathematical computation. Both below- and on-grade-level readers may need targeted instruction with these words.

Standardized assessments use academic language such as *summarize, infer, conclude, numerator, denominator, sum,* and so forth. To be successful on standardized assessments, students need automaticity with academic language found there to understand what is being asked of them. Academic language includes content-specific terms like *octagon* and *quadrilateral.* These content vocabulary examples may seem obvious. What is less obvious is the academic language that includes terms such as *trace, inference, cause and effect, sequence,* and *conclusion.* Teachers must be careful to directly instruct academic language, use academic language in class, and expect students to use academic language so that they own and understand the language when it is encountered during assessment or independent content area reading (Feldman & Kinsella, 2004).

Beyond the automaticity or immediate understanding of basic vocabulary, students need strategies for solving vocabulary challenges. Studying root words, prefixes, and suffixes provides students with tools for solving questions about meaning. Did you know that about 56% of the English language is based on Latin? Given that more than half of the commonly used words in English are derived from Latin, learning Latin roots, prefixes, and suffixes will be helpful in creating students who are savvy vocabulary solvers. All students have an edge with this type of word study, but English-as-a-second-language students whose home language is derived from Latin—Spanish, Portuguese, Italian, and French—make rapid growth in English vocabulary acquisition (Bellamo, 2005). It connects to their prior language experience and provides a basis for scaffolding to English-language learning at a higher level.

A smaller percentage, about 16% of English, is based on Greek, and a little less is based on German. Content teachers are encouraged to identify roots, prefixes, and suffixes that appear in their textbooks and teach them directly. This will be more helpful to students than the assignment of memorizing vocabulary lists.

VOCABULARY IN CONTEXT

Learning vocabulary in context is often the first suggestion students are given for solving challenging vocabulary. Let's find the target word, **precipice**, in context in the sentence that follows. Underline the meaning as it is given in the sentence.

> The **precipice**, an awesome *high cliff,* was so straight and rugged with rocks that it forbade us from climbing up the mountain any farther.

Precipice is boldfaced, and I have *italicized* the meaning in the sentence.

Students are taught in intermediate grades to determine the meaning from context clues. In this case, it works fairly easily, but as students read more difficult and technical nonfiction and informational text, there are fewer context clues to assist them.

Content textbooks tend to have the word defined the first time the word shows up, or it is highlighted or **boldfaced**, then followed by a definition. Glance at a mathematics, science, or social studies textbook to verify this. Point out to students how the textbook is organized to support their vocabulary development in this way. Below-grade-level readers have difficulty understanding vocabulary using context clues.

Teachers understand textbook organization and often attend professional development seminars on how new textbooks are organized and how to use them most effectively. Honor the students by taking time to do the same for them. Demystify textbooks for students!

Here is another passage. What would make sense for the word **nylons** to mean in this sentence?

> "Sally is the girl with eyes like Egypt and nylons the color of smoke." (Sally, in *The House on Mango Street* by Sandra Cisneros.)

If I'm twelve years old, I may not know what nylon is or what nylons are. I cannot really determine the meaning of nylons from the sentence so I need other strategies. If I look in the glossary of the book where I found the story, I do not find *nylons*. My next strategy is to go to a dictionary, where I find "*Nylon: a strong, elastic, artificial (man-made) fiber.*"

As a twelve-year-old, I ask myself, "What could she have of man-made fiber the color of smoke?" If I have not figured out what it means by now, I may ask a friend, "What are nylons?"

As a teacher leading a class discussion, I may teach the students a vocabulary strategy for thinking through meanings called "word questioning." It has been used effectively with students in Grades 4–12 across content curriculum. I would ask the class to generate responses to these questions or make a graphic organizer to be completed by students and used as a visual for teaching, modeling, and practicing word questioning.

WORD QUESTIONING TARGET WORD: *NYLONS*

1. What could it mean? *Some of her clothing or something she has*

2. What could it not mean? *Any human part because it is man-made*

3. What could it be like? *Pantyhose, stockings*

4. Where else could I find this word? *Movies, books, stories in which the settings are before about 1980*

5. Substitute *pantyhose* or *stockings* in the sentence.

6. Does the sentence make sense?

7. If it makes sense, write a definition for nylons in your own words.

8. Personal Definition: Nylons are like stockings or pantyhose and are made of a man-made fabric called nylon.

9. Add a nonlinguistic representation of "nylons."

Now I may ask students to compare our personal definition with one in a dictionary. The key is a personal definition, not a memorized one that someone else wrote. Ownership of vocabulary—personal understanding and use—develops students into expert readers, writers, and content learners.

TEXTBOOK VOCABULARY LISTS

Textbooks have vocabulary lists for each chapter. Sometimes these lists are in the beginning of the chapter and sometimes at the end. As already mentioned, in science or social studies, the lists can have as many as 30 words. What can a teacher do if she knows that students need to understand vocabulary before they can read fluently and comprehend the text when there are so many new words?

Keep in mind that a student can keep only 3 to 7 new pieces of information in his working memory at any one time. New vocabulary is new information. So how many new words should be introduced at any one time? Yes, 3–7, or about 5. Teachers are encouraged to scrutinize the vocabulary and select the 5 or so words most essential to initial understanding of the new content or words the students are least likely to know, given what the teacher knows about the students. Teach and use those words until the students demonstrate understanding, then introduce the next 5–7, and continue until all essential vocabulary is understood, even as many as 20 or 30 words. This is called "chunking" the vocabulary. It may be that students already know some of the words or perhaps do not really need to know all of them. This is teacher decision making rather than the textbook driving the vocabulary learning decisions.

Another strategy regarding the content chapter vocabulary is to look for commonalities. Chunk the vocabulary into common groupings. For instance, words with common roots, prefixes, and suffixes could be grouped together for making connections and creating rapid understanding. *Physiology, psychology, biology,* and *gynecology* may all be grouped together to discover meanings by recognizing word parts. When I was visiting a local school, the life science teacher stopped me in the hallway to share that his students had been studying all of the "ology" words that day. Assisting students in making explicit connections to groups of words, their relationships, and commonalities develops ownership of vocabulary.

Word Parts

Ask students,

1. "What part(s) of the word do you recognize?"

2. "What does that word part(s) mean?"

3. "What do you think that word means?"

4. "Write the definition in your own words."

If you believe that students must know the textbook definition or your definition, then after writing those definitions, ask them to put the meaning in their own words. Following their personal definition should be their nonlinguistic representation. These extra steps are essential for student ownership of the vocabulary. It is a lower-level task for a student to copy or even memorize a definition than the higher-level task of putting the definition in "my own words" and creating a nonlinguistic representation.

Mental Model: Vocabulary Solvers

The concept of developing vocabulary solvers was modeled effectively by several different content area teachers (English, mathematics, science, and social studies) I visited recently in a high school. Each teacher had "today's vocabulary" posted on his or her whiteboard. The range of vocabulary was from 2 to 5, reasonable for daily introduction. Each teacher asked the students to think about what the words meant and generate possible meanings based on prior knowledge. The students were directed to the use of the vocabulary in the text to further clarify meaning and use. After class discussion, students wrote in their notebooks the meanings *in their own words.*

WORD WALLS

Creating a literacy-rich environment includes visual depictions of vocabulary. In the earliest grades, word walls are often composed of the alphabet with lists of words learned and students' names on a wall in the classroom. This can be helpful in primary grades or in intensive reading intervention as sound and symbol relationships are being developed and the teacher wants automaticity in recognizing and pronouncing frequently occurring words.

From Grades 4 and up, words alone on a wall are not helpful, except to identify that there are many content words and that if I am a below-grade-level reader, I may not know them all. The literacy tasks at this level are vocabulary, fluency, and comprehension. To this end, word walls should support comprehension of content text. Positive examples include words and their meanings. Even better are words, meanings, visuals, and examples in a sentence. These types of word walls assist students with making connections of prior knowledge to new learning and to make sense of related concepts and words.

Variations on word walls are mind maps showing relationships of parts to whole, concepts, and systems. Another example would be word walls related to word families. Resource word walls, like roots, prefixes, and suffixes, help students to own vocabulary strategies. Use the word walls as resources within the instructional plans. Refer to them when a student encounters a difficult word. Use the word walls to create automaticity in vocabulary solving.

Encourage student development of the word walls so that they own them and find them to be personal resources. This will support the students in becoming independent vocabulary solvers.

Mental Model: Personal Word Wall

While visiting a world history classroom, I observed the teacher introducing seven new vocabulary words. Then the students wrote the word, defined it, and created a visual on an $8\frac{1}{2} \times 11$-inch-size paper for each word. Students used colorful or white paper, markers, and colored pencils provided by the teacher and placed on a table in the front of the room. I noticed that the students not only wrote the words, but wrote them with creative flair and seemed to have fun while taking the task seriously. As is my practice while in a classroom, I invited one of the young ladies to explain the assignment since it occurred to me that writing definitions in her notebook would be faster. The young, but wise, student explained to me that when you write the word, what it means to you, and a sketch representing the word, you remember its definition. "Then what happens?" I asked. She responded that the teacher collects all seven sheets from each student, selects one sheet for each word, and posts it on the classroom word wall. The others are returned to the students, and they place them in their notebook section My Personal Word Wall. While I admit I was impressed with the process, I really wanted to know the result, if any, of it, so I asked the resident expert student, "Did this process make any difference in learning the new vocabulary?" Emphatically she responded that it did and that her grades were much improved.

PERSONAL DICTIONARY, THESAURUS, OR JOURNAL

The theme of creating student ownership of vocabulary continues to arise. Here it is again with the idea of each student developing a personal dictionary, thesaurus, or journal in each content classroom. In the mathematics journal, students place notes for the day, examples of terms, and steps in problem solving. The front the journal will have a table of contents to which students will add entries as they develop their journals. It will become their personal resource for mathematics.

Students will place the vocabulary that they have been asked to take note of in their personal dictionary or thesaurus. In addition, there will be sections on "words I think are interesting," "words I like," and "words I've learned." A world geography teacher asks students to identify "cool words," followed by class discussion. From these cool words, the vocabulary for further study is selected by the teacher.

These headings are positive and allow the student to be accountable for his or her own vocabulary acquisition. Some teachers find that asking students to identify "words I don't know" continues to work, but others find that middle and high school students begin to resist negative labels. Try different labels and determine what is most successful with your unique group of students. Sources for these vocabulary words may be the shared reading, read-alouds, textbooks, accountable independent reading, or other reading and instruction.

What makes these resources particularly useful is that the vocabulary is unique to each student and respects the student's developmental stage. One of the negatives of standard vocabulary lists and vocabulary workbooks is that the prescription is the same for each student. Just as excellent vocabulary software would assess and individually prescribe for each student personal lists in small chunks, students create their own personal resources. Students enjoy developing their own resources rather than always having standard resources.

VOCABULARY WORKBOOKS

When I am with middle and high school faculty and administrators, one of the most frequently asked questions is, "What do you think about vocabulary workbooks?" The reason this question is asked is that generations of college-bound students have had vocabulary workbooks to complete each week, the purpose of which is to prepare them to take college entrance examinations. Therefore, vocabulary workbooks are part of the school culture in many middle and high schools, particularly those with successful college-bound students.

The positive angle of vocabulary workbooks is that they do not hurt students and they ensure that students are being introduced to new vocabulary. On the negative side, the research on vocabulary acquisition is clear that words need to be used in context and multiple times (as many as 30 for average students or 500 for struggling ones!) in reading, writing, and speaking before they are owned. Few vocabulary workbooks present words in context, but rather they present words as new lists for the week. Exercises include fill in the blanks, multiple choice for meaning, analogies, antonyms, and synonyms. If you wander into any middle or high school cafeteria at lunch, you will see students frantically completing the assignments before English class, or, heaven forbid, copying a fellow student's answers.

Let me try to offer a solution. If the school's culture and community expect vocabulary workbooks, then select a language arts or literature anthology that has a companion vocabulary workbook. This way, the vocabulary study will most likely connect to the reading and writing designed by the publisher.

One school was using an anthology from one publisher and a vocabulary workbook from another. Even though the vocabulary workbook attempted to make connections to literature, the students were using another publisher's literature text, and therefore the connections were useless. To exacerbate the vocabulary workbook issue and in the name of rigor, ninth- and tenth-grade students who were advanced used the eleventh- and twelfth-grade versions of the workbook series, ensuring lack of connection to literature read, discussed, and written about even if the vocabulary workbook and literature text had the same publisher—which was not the case. What this example shows is that well-meaning educators who care about vocabulary acquisition really believe that vocabulary practice in isolation can improve student achievement, but it does not.

Mental Model: Linking Vocabulary Workbooks to Literature

Gloria Johnson, an insightful literacy coach, provided the teachers with examples of assessment items that can assist the teacher in linking the vocabulary to the passages currently being read, discussed, and written about. Here are some of the examples she has provided to teachers to use as models. You will see that she is asking the students to apply the new vocabulary to themselves and to the text read, using thinking and writing. This is an excellent literacy strategy called "making connections." These types of questions are at higher thinking levels than those generally found in vocabulary workbooks, and because they connect to the reading passages, to the students, and to the world, students are more likely to move the vocabulary from short-term to long-term memory, or to actually improve their vocabulary. If you use nonliterature-based vocabulary workbooks, think about ways like this example to connect the vocabulary to classroom reading, discussion, and writing. The boldfaced target words are from the vocabulary workbook assigned to students.

- Describe something you **negotiated** with someone else. Be sure to include two specific details.
- How did Odysseus remain **inconspicuous** after he returned to Ithaca? Support your answer with evidence.
- What **demoralizes** you? Give three reasons to support your answer.
- Name the **landlocked** country you would most like to visit and explain why you selected that country.
- Which two **extremities** of the Mediterranean world were visited by Odysseus? Describe why these locations were dangerous.

SPELLING AND WRITING

There is a relationship between student achievement in spelling and achievement in reading comprehension. This does not mean that students need spelling lists and tests each week, but it does mean that they should spell correctly in their writing in Grades 4 and up. With the accessibility of resources for spelling, students should be encouraged to check their work and edit as needed. As students learn new vocabulary, visualize the new vocabulary, and put the meaning into their own words, they should also become spellers of the new vocabulary in the context of their writing.

Direct instruction on the rules of spelling continues to be effective in providing students with a spelling resource. Learning homophones like *dear* and *deer* or *their* and *there* are helpful strategies. There are also commonly confused words that sound very much alike, such as *annul, anal,* and *annual,* in which direction instruction can benefit students. We have already discussed learning roots, prefixes, and suffixes, which is also a spelling strategy. Don't forget those word walls. Remember that they can focus on any of these strategies—rules, homophones, confusing words, roots, prefixes, and suffixes. Along with developing vocabulary solvers, we want students to be able to spell the vocabulary and use it correctly in speaking and writing.

PRACTICAL TIPS FOR DEVELOPING STUDENT-OWNED VOCABULARY

Tips for Grades 4–12 English, Reading, Language Arts, and Content Areas

- Students should read, read, read, read, read, read, read a variety of texts.

- Use all the processes of literacy in introducing new vocabulary: reading, writing, speaking, listening, viewing, thinking, and multiple-symbol systems.
- Use new vocabulary in multiple ways as many as 30 times.
- Ask students to define in their own words and illustrate the word on a 5 × 7 card; post the card on the bulletin board. Or—students make their own personal word wall in their notebooks.
- Think of the word that best represents the topic being studied. Write it on a card. Ask students to form small groups and make a concept map of the cards showing relationships of each of the words to one another. Post the concept maps and share them. Students will have built on prior knowledge and expanded vocabulary.
- Before reading the text, give pairs of students cards with one word on each card. The students are to decide what the word means and then how to teach it to the other students through role-playing, demonstration, art, and so on. Each pair teaches the word to the remainder of the class, and no one will forget the meanings!
- Ask students to look at the concept map. What three conclusions can they draw from the concept map? Share with your neighbor. Add your neighbor's conclusions to your list if they are different from yours.
- Vocabulary Sort: Print vocabulary on one color of paper and definitions on another color. Cut out each vocabulary and definition. Place one complete set in a bag, making enough bags for each pair of students in the class. Give each pair of students a bag of words and definitions. Give them 5 minutes to sort the vocabulary and definitions. After 5 minutes, tell the students to take out their notes and textbook and find the ones that were not matched and check those they think are correct.

Tips for Grades 4–12 English, Language Arts, Reading, and Intensive Reading

- For 1 minute list all the words that sound like, or are in the category of, or are a synonym for, antonym for, homophone for _____ .
- Take 2 minutes and list all the prefixes and suffixes that you can think of. Then for 2 minutes compare them to your neighbor's. Now take 1 minute and write what each means.

(Continued)

(Continued)

- Popcorn Vocabulary: Give each student a card with a new word and meaning. Each student reads orally for the class the word and meaning. Time how long it takes for the class to complete the readings. Do this each day and chart how the speed increases working on vocabulary and fluency. Create a competition in increasing speed among classes of the same content and grade.
- Ask students to close their eyes and visualize the word wall of roots, prefixes, and suffixes. How many words can they make with what they visualize? Compare your list to your partner's for 2 minutes. Question any words that do not seem to make sense or that you are not sure of.
- Below-grade-level readers: After providing a short list of vocabulary words, ask the students to rate each word based on their prior knowledge. Discussing their ratings provides a quick assessment of what they know. Use the discussion to introduce each word and its meaning.

1 = I know the word and its meaning.

2 = I know the word, but I am not sure of the meaning.

3 = I have seen the word, but I do not know what it means.

4 = I have never seen the word.

Developing Fluency in Reading All Texts

As introduced in Chapter 2, for most students in Grades 4 and up, the literacy components needing emphases are vocabulary, fluency, and comprehension. Most reading, language arts, and English teachers attend to vocabulary acquisition and comprehension skill development. Teachers of other content (such as mathematics, science, the arts, vocational and technical education, and social studies) see themselves as also teaching vocabulary and may not directly teach reading, but they expect reading comprehension of their content text. The literacy component most often overlooked in Grades 4 and up, including in reading classes, is oral reading fluency.

WHAT IS FLUENCY AND WHY IS IT SO IMPORTANT?

Anything we do fluently we do effortlessly and smoothly with an appropriate rate. Lance Armstrong rides a bicycle fluently, Josh Groban sings fluently, and Jennifer Lopez dances fluently. Those who read fluently do so with smoothness, expression, correct phrasing, and appropriate rate so that oral reading sounds like the reader understands the text.

Students may have the misunderstanding that fluency or good reading is fast reading. This misunderstanding, which should be corrected, comes from being timed during the primary school years. Students take away the message and generalize that faster at anything is better. In contrast to fast reading, fluent reading is smooth, with appropriate phrasing and conversational pace. Reading fluently is reading with an appropriate rate that communicates understanding of the passage.

Generally, a student reads fluently if he or she reads on-grade-level texts with 90%–95% accuracy. A quick check on the fluency of a student is to ask the student to read an on-grade-level text for 60 seconds. If the student has few errors and reads smoothly, you are safe in assuming the student reads with fluency. I always suggest following up that 1-minute read with, "How would you summarize what you just read?" We never want to leave students with the impression that rate and accuracy in pronunciation are enough; comprehension is the goal, and comprehension is how reading will be measured on standardized assessments.

While in a high school intensive reading intervention classroom, I was reminded of why this is important. I listened while a student read beautifully and recorded a passage for the teacher to listen to. When I commented on how fluently he read, the student responded, "Oh, yes, I read well. I just don't understand it." We tend to think of below-grade-level readers as those who are not articulate, but middle-class students who live in literacy-rich environments sometimes arrive at middle and high school without comprehension skills and mask them with their middle-class conversation and compliant behavior. Always checking for comprehension and never assuming comprehension are essential to improving readers, writers, and content learners.

Before a student can read fluently, he must know the vocabulary and be able to decode it effortlessly. Otherwise, the reading will have stops and starts with the cognitive effort or working memory consumed with pronunciation (NICHD, 2000). Once the student can decode the words effortlessly and knows their meaning, he can work to reflect punctuation marks appropriately and purposefully emphasize particular words or phrases.

There is a relationship between low fluency and students who have difficulty with comprehension (Pinnell, Pikulski, Wixson, Campbell, Gough, & Beatty, 1995). When fluency is achieved, then the cognitive effort or working memory is available to attend to comprehension—the goal of reading. Making working memory available for comprehension is the reason fluency in reading all texts in all classrooms is important.

Fluency in reading **all** texts is important, not just fiction. Does the English teacher want the students to read the anthology fluently? Of course she does. Do the mathematics, science, and social studies teachers want their students to read their texts fluently? Yes, they do also. If teachers of all classes want their students to read their texts fluently and with comprehension, then each should address fluency in reading his or her particular textbooks since each is different. Students who read below grade level will have limited access to the on-grade-level content within the textbook unless each of their teachers addresses fluency with that textbook.

It is easier than it sounds. Basically, fluency is developed through hearing fluent models, reading, and rereading. In the next two sections, instructional strategies are offered for enhancing fluency in reading intervention and standards-based content classes in Grades 4–12.

DEVELOPING FLUENCY IN READING INTERVENTION

Reading intervention classes include intensive reading (those reading below grade level), reading for second-language students, and reading for special education students. While each of these classifications has uniqueness, each one should work directly on reading fluently for those who read below grade level, and particularly readers in the lowest quartile on standardized assessments. Working directly on fluency should be done in a respectful manner appropriate to the age and developmental stage of the student.

Directly teach, model, and practice with students the vocabulary word *fluency*, or *reading fluently*. You may want to use the Fluency Scale in Figure 4.1 or another one to provide a graphic organizer related to reading fluency. Within the Fluency Scale are vocabulary words that may need clarification as well as teaching. This direct teaching of what reading fluency means will clarify any misconceptions the student may have related to what good readers do. Students as young as six years old have explained to me what fluent reading means and have told me what they do to improve their reading fluency. Older students should be able to do the same.

While developing an understanding of fluency, the teacher should model fluent reading for the students to hear. This is aligned with the daily nonnegotiable of reading to and with students. Be explicit with students, asking them why you paused at certain moments, why you lifted your voice, or why you emphasized certain words or phrases. A variety of fiction and nonfiction including poetry, essays, expository writing, and persuasive texts should be used to model fluency. The purpose is to model reading different kinds of texts in different ways.

Keep in mind that only fluent readers should be reading out loud to the entire class—the teacher, compact disk, DVD, or audiotape. Why am I insistent that nonfluent readers not read out loud to the class? In an intervention classroom where students are generally nonfluent, inaccurate oral reading creates more misunderstandings of sound and symbol relationships and does not advance reading fluency and comprehension. On the other hand, when the teacher is working with small guided reading groups she may want to ask students to read out loud while supporting their improvement in fluency.

Reading Intervention Whole-Class Fluency Strategies

Another daily nonnegotiable is to teach, model, and practice strategies of expert readers and writers. Anything we want students to do well we teach, model, and practice until they can perform the task independently and own the strategy. Fluency strategies are no different from comprehension strategies. There are a number of fluency strategies that are easy to incorporate into the intervention classroom and take only a few minutes. Each one of these includes fluent modeling and/or practice before a student reads to the class. Following are some examples that have been used successfully in Grades 4–12:

- When reading to students, model rereading a confusing or particularly interesting passage. Model rereading for comprehension, clarification, and enjoyment.
- Students read a passage to a partner and then reverse who reads.
- After the teacher models reading a passage or poem, the class reads chorally the same passage.
- The teacher reads a passage, and then the students read chorally the next passage.
- Students practice reading a passage independently, with a parent or a student partner, then read for the class.
- Students record themselves reading a passage and then listen to it, reread it, and record it until it gets better based on a fluency scale.
- Students practice reading an appropriate passage with another student and record the time it takes. After practice, students repeat the timing of the reading. Caution students that the timing is secondary to the smoothness, phrasing, and expression and should improve with practice until the reading is conversational.

You may note that all of these strategies are alternatives to round-robin reading (reading without practice student by student), which many teachers mistakenly use to give oral reading practice. Why is round-robin reading not recommended? (Because nonfluent readers read out loud, confusing other nonfluent readers, and the reader has not had time to practice and receive feedback [Stallings, 1980].)

Reading Intervention: Differentiating Fluency Instruction

Intervention classes should maximize use of research-based literacy practice, including differentiated instruction. In addition to whole-class instruction as we may typically see, intervention teachers should work with small groups of students and with individuals as needed. Note that this does not refer to students working in cooperative groups but to the teacher working with six or fewer students for a period of time, maybe 15–20 minutes of a class period, while the rest of the students work individually, at centers, or in small student groups.

These small groups working with the teacher may be determined because they have either similar independent reading levels, or similar skill needs, or are reading the same book, a book by the same author, or a book on the same theme. Perhaps the teacher is working on the reading-writing connection and groups students with similar writing support needs. These small groups should be developed strategically by the teacher and not selected by the students.

From the fluency-building perspective, this small-group time is when the teacher is working with up to six students using fluency strategies and giving specific feedback and coaching to individual students. Most students do not get to have such personal time with a teacher and such personal and immediate correctives and encouragement. In a three-year study of literacy intervention classrooms in a large, diverse, urban district, the middle school students were consistent in voicing that their favorite time of the class was the small-group time with the teacher (Coney, 1996). This rating may be a surprise, as small-group time was more preferable than technology time, whole-class time, or accountable independent reading time.

Just as students benefit from direct instruction within the whole class and from strategic small-group instruction, coveted time is that individual time with a teacher. While this is very difficult to achieve, teachers are encouraged to schedule individual time with each student periodically. During this time, you may listen to a student read a passage and score his fluency. This is also a wonderful time to show him a graphic of his fluency in August or September and how it has developed, along with his reading comprehension level. You may have listened to a short recording of his oral reading, and you want to play it back for him and allow him to self-monitor and correct. Fluency development takes reading and rereading along with continual listening to fluent readings of texts.

Using a Fluency Scale

You may find that using a fluency scale with students is effective. Teach, model, and practice using a scale. Introduce the fluency scale and model reading. Ask them to rate you first on each component and then on the whole. Select a passage that is no more than two years above the students' independent reading comprehension levels so they can read fairly easily with you. You will probably want to practice the reading of the passage before class and purposefully make a few errors for them to note. If students can rate you, then they demonstrate understanding of fluency. Developing this level of understanding will assist students in improving their own fluency when you ask them to explicitly focus on it for a few minutes.

As an example, you may give the students an on-grade-level passage to read. First, the teacher should read it to the students, modeling fluent reading while they follow along (reading with). Then the class may read the passage chorally together. Third, the students should read and reread individually until they are ready to read orally to the teacher or a peer and be given feedback using the Fluency Scale or another scale of your choice. You may do this on Monday, then again on Wednesday, and by Friday the score should be moving up toward the maximum of 4 if you are working on one component or 16 if you are working on all four components. This type of safe practice and fluency development will motivate students as they are able to chart their improvement day by day.

DEVELOPING FLUENCY IN READING CONTENT TEXTS

Textbooks in standards-based curriculum content classrooms challenge students reading below grade level. Content textbooks are written on grade level or above. Often they are written to support a curriculum, not a grade level. If the English, mathematics, science, or social studies classroom has students who cannot read the text fluently, then it is suggested that teachers infuse fluency strategies into their instructional practice.

Assessing Fluency With the Textbook

How will a teacher know if the student can read the text fluently? There are several methods that will take a little time at the beginning of the year. First, if you are not provided comprehension levels of the students you receive in your classes, make that request to the appropriate person: data coach, literacy coach, counselor, assistant principal, or principal. Once you have identified those students who appear to be reading below grade level, ask them to record a paragraph of oral reading from the textbook. It will not matter what page or chapter since the entire textbook will be written on one reading level. This could take 1 minute per student and could be accomplished in one class period. If you do not have access to reading comprehension data, then you may want to ask every student to record a paragraph for you. This tape can be listened to in a relatively short period of time.

Figure 4.1   Fluency Scale

	Date:	Date:	Date:
Student: _____ Passage to be read and reread: _____			
	Score 1–4	Score 1–4	Score 1–4
Phrasing			
1 = monitor, little sense of phrase, word-by-word reading			
2 = frequent 2–3 word phrases, choppy, improper stress, intonation, fails to mark ends of sentences			
3 = run-ons, midsentence pauses for breath, reasonable stress/intonation			
4 = well phrased, mostly in clause and sentence units, adequate expression			
Smoothness			
1 = frequent extended pauses, hesitations, false starts, sound-outs, repetitions			
2 = several extended pauses, hesitations, disruptive			
3 = occasional breaks in smoothness caused by difficulties with specific words or structures			
4 = generally smooth reading with some breaks, but word and structure difficulties are resolved with *self-correction*			
Pace			
1 = slow and laborious			
2 = moderately slow			
3 = uneven mixture of fast and slow reading			
4 = consistently conversational			
Expression and Voice			
1 = quiet, monotone voice			
2 = emphasis on pronouncing words, some natural language			
3 = volume and expression natural, occasionally monotone			
4 = good expression, volume aligned with comprehension			
Total Score for Each Reading			

SOURCE: Based on Zutell & Rasinski, 1991.

Ask any student whose fluency you question to read an on-grade-level textbook for 60 seconds. A sixth-grade student should read about 160 words per minute in an on-grade-level textbook with no more than a few errors. Does the student read smoothly with no more than a few errors?

Either way, students who are not fluent readers of the textbook will be obvious. You may use the Fluency Scale to score each student, but it really is not necessary. Listen for smooth conversational reading with only a few errors that sounds as if the student understands what is being read. Ask the student to explain to you the 60-second read. If the student is successful, you can expect that he will be able to read the textbook independently with comprehension.

Textbook Fluency Strategies

Once you have identified who cannot read the textbook fluently, you will have a place to begin providing support with vocabulary, fluency, and comprehension. Since vocabulary has already been addressed and comprehension will have in-depth discussion in Chapter 5, here we will focus primarily on fluency-building strategies. You may want to refer to the fluency strategies identified in the section Developing Fluency in Reading Intervention. Strategic use of fluency strategies early in the term will yield benefits as the term progresses. It may be that you will see an improvement of fluency and comprehension of the textbook as the term proceeds, and you can reduce the use of fluency strategies. These strategies are alternatives to round-robin reading and are appropriate for Grades 4–12.

The most encouraged strategy is to read to and with the students. This does not mean the entire chapter, but selected essential passages. Recall that students' oral language comprehension is about 2 years advanced of their print language comprehension, and you are modeling how to read the textbook. Following is a strategy to use with any textbook at any grade level:

1. First, identify short passages that are essential for understanding the chapter. These probably include the first paragraph, last paragraph, and a few others within the chapter.

2. Ask students to turn to the passage and follow along while you read it orally.

3. Then, ask the students to read it chorally with you. Choral reading is safe reading for those who struggle.

4. Next, ask for volunteers to point out vocabulary in the passage that is important for comprehending the passage. The students should explain the vocabulary as well as identify the words.

5. Students should now read the passage individually and silently.

6. Ask a volunteer to give the main idea of the passage.

7. After reviewing the essential passages, ask the students to read the remainder of the text section independently.

These steps work on vocabulary, fluency, and comprehension—which develop together. This is quick and effective regardless of grade level or content area.

Another strategy is to provide a passage below grade level that addresses the same standards-based curriculum content that you are going to read in the textbook. Reading this passage will build background knowledge, vocabulary, and fluency in reading about the target concept and content. After developing interest, vocabulary, and understanding of the below-grade-level passage, scaffold the students to the on-grade-level textbook passage on the same concepts.

A variation on this strategy is to select a targeted topic or concept passage out of your local newspaper or *USA Today*. Select the same targeted topic or concept passage from the *New York Times*, which will be on a higher reading level. Students read the easier passage, then read the more difficult one. Reading the easier passage first should assist in reading fluently and comprehending the more difficult one. Follow the reading with comprehension skills such as author's purpose, point of view, comparison, inferences, or conclusions. Scaffold from these contemporary texts to the textbook passages on the same topic or concept.

Partner reading works well for building fluency and comprehension of textbook passages. Students are assigned a partner or choose one. (One of the two should be a better reader.) Give each pair a section of the chapter to read and reread to each other until it is being read fluently. The better reader should read first. Reading and rereading should take about 5 minutes. The pairs develop a 1-sentence summary of each paragraph assigned taking another 5 minutes. After the partner reading and 1-sentence summary development, class discussion of the chapter with the pairs taking the lead for their sections proceeds. One-sentence summaries may be written on transparencies, sentence strips, or chart paper and shared with the class (perhaps posted), providing a sequence or outline of the chapter. All students note the vocabulary and 1-sentence summaries. Some teachers provide a structured note-taking template for writing these down for each section. Chemistry teachers reported to me that this approach created greater engagement and resulted in higher grades than previous years' lecturing with PowerPoint presentations, note taking, and discussion.

Provide options for students to have fluent oral models for their independent reading. If the textbook has a companion DVD or audiotape, set up a listening station or center in the classroom for the student, as mentioned in Chapter 2. An option is to allow students to check out the technology support to use at home when reading independently. You will be pleased with the positive difference these cost-effective technology solutions make in student fluency and comprehension of the textbook content.

ACCOUNTABLE INDEPENDENT READING

Fluency is developed with practice. To own literacy strategies, a student has to practice. Accountable independent reading is one in which the student practices the fluency, vocabulary solving, and literacy strategies that the teacher has been teaching and modeling for him. Accountable independent reading is the fifth nonnegotiable expectation of daily practice. The other four create the conditions for and the experience to become a better reader, writer, and content learner. The fifth nonnegotiable is when the student practices to get better. How often do you think Lance Armstrong rides his bicycle? It has been said that he rides every day between 6 and 13 hours. That is why he is a fluent cyclist. It would be nice if students read 6 hours per day, but a minimum of 20 minutes each day is recommended for students to read independently with accountability to improve vocabulary, fluency, and comprehension.

You are invited to consider some parameters that enhance the growth that will be experienced by these consistent applications of accountable independent reading.

1. Students have choice of respectful books.

2. Match students to texts.

3. Students read books, not other print, for accountability.

4. Accountability is friendly.

5. At least 50% of the books read for accountable independent reading are nonfiction.

Choice

Choice is a motivator for students, and it becomes more so as they enter adolescence. The teacher responsible for accountable independent reading should have a classroom library that represents the reading range and interests of the students. Look back in Chapter 1, in the section Nonnegotiable 1: Literacy-Rich and Print-Rich Classrooms, to review the classroom library. Asking the students to take a quick interest survey will assist the teacher in providing books that are likely to engage the students.

These texts should also be developmentally appropriate and respectful of the student. This means that the books should be written by authors and have characters in the books to whom the students can relate. One of the most popular new series of adolescent literature is the *Bluford Series* by Townsend Press. These books are written with African American adolescents in mind and reflect these young people in the characters and in the themes. Students love the *Bluford Series* regardless of their ethnic background. A student recently commented to a reading intervention teacher, "You must really love us to get us these books!" This sentiment is reflected in the community of learners as students realize that the classroom library is carefully designed with each of them in mind.

For below-grade-level readers, there are excellent collections available from most publishers that support the science and social studies standards and are engaging. The *X Zone* offered by the Wright Group is respectful of the interests of older students, particularly boys—such as cars, sports, and outdoors activities. These selections are targeting students in Grades 4–6, and the readability is about third-grade level. The more students read nonfiction or fiction with nonfiction vocabulary and concepts, the better they will perform on reading comprehension sections of assessments since the majority of items relate to science and social studies.

Think about asking the librarian to pull together a collection of 50 books on the reading levels of your students and on the concepts being studied. Check these out and then get another collection when the concepts you are teaching change. The librarian at Sebastian River High School increased circulation tremendously to the point where she created a classroom library of 200 books on a cart for each ninth-grade English teacher. The books reflected a range of reading levels and interest areas, all appropriate for 14- to 15-year-old students. Students check these books out directly from their English teacher, who holds them accountable for the reading. Reading comprehension at Sebastian River High School is graphing positively each year!

Matching Students to Texts

This phrase, matching students to texts, refers to the teacher knowing the independent reading levels of the students and the reading levels of the books in the classroom library. By knowing the reading levels of the books, we are referring to knowing the grade-level equivalent or a school-used measure such as the Lexile of the book. The important point is that both the student data and the text readability should be noted with the same language—grade level, Lexile, or other methods. When the teacher knows the student's interest and reading level, then the student can be guided to selections that match both interest and reading level, with the student making the final selection.

Mental Model: Matching Students to Text

At the end of the school day, I commented to an intensive reading teacher how engaged the students were and the obvious positive relationship she had with them. I also acknowledged the displays of beautiful books and the classroom library. Angel, the intensive reading teacher, shared with me that after she gets to know the students, she will browse through the school's library or Barnes and Noble just previewing books, looking for ones that will engage specific struggling students. When she finds the perfect book, she will take it to the student and let him or her know that it was selected just for the individual. This kind of commitment on the part of the teacher to match students to texts results in the engagement of the older struggling reader and measurable improvement in reading.

Other Independent Reading

There are many types of independent reading. Accountable independent reading refers to students reading books and being held accountable for doing so. Reading other print such as magazines, newsletters, newspapers, and so forth can be interesting and engage the reader, but the accountability is difficult to measure. Many students who are two or more years below grade level in their reading have not been held accountable for reading books. Well-meaning teachers have allowed the students to read anything, as long as they were reading or acting as if they were. These teachers thought that if the students had their eyes on print and the print was a topic of interest, it would help the student to improve in reading. Reading something is better than reading nothing, but books are best if you want to improve reading levels and create lifelong readers. When I visit high school reading intervention classes, I find that most of the students never read a book until their intervention teacher said it was nonnegotiable and assisted them in finding that perfect beginning book. Once they find that perfect beginning book, they read and reread and begin to improve in their reading vocabulary, fluency, and comprehension.

I wonder how these students would be reading if reading a book had been nonnegotiable for them throughout elementary and middle school.

Accountability Is Friendly

Accountability after reading a book is in place in most schools for student reading. Typically, it is a quiz or the book report. Both of these are a breeze for on-grade-level readers, and both are challenging, maybe too challenging for the below-grade-level reader. When standing behind students who are taking book quizzes on books that I've never read, I find that I can answer most questions accurately because the thinking level represented is low.

When determining the accountability measure that you will accept, ask yourself, "What is the purpose of accountable independent reading?" In the fail-safe classroom, the purpose is to give students practice in reading so they will read more and become better readers. If the accountability is not something with which the student can be successful, say, a quiz, then the accountability may interfere with the student reading more—the purpose of accountable independent reading. Because of the history of accountability turning students off to reading, many experts say just read, read, read, and do not hold students accountable. The fail-safe point of view is that teachers need documentation of reading books and charting growth, and that this documentation is motivating to students and cause for celebration!

Since we want book completion accountability to be friendly, what are some possible choices? In Grades 4–12, making mobiles, book jackets, book advertisements, book talks, and flip charts are just a few. Book talks to the teacher, the class, or others in the school may be an option. If the characters are particularly interesting, perhaps the student will make a character map of his favorite character and write why he selected that particular character. As a teacher, determine several types of accountability that you will accept and allow the students to choose from those several which one to use. In addition to being friendly, it should relate to practice of targeted comprehension skills, as the examples given do (summary, main idea/supporting details, fact/opinion, cause/effect, comparison, contrast, inference, literary elements), or comprehension strategies (prediction/clarification, evaluation, visualization, connections, questions). A word of caution: It is common to limit accountability to literacy elements, and yet minimal items on standardized assessments relate to literary elements. Teach, model, and practice all comprehension skills and strategies equally. A sample Book Talk Checklist is found in Resources.

In addition to accountability after completing the book, day-by-day accountability is important. At the end of the 20- to 30-minute reading time, ask the students to enter into their reading log information such as date, ending page, and 1–2 sentences that reflect what took place. These 1–2 sentences reflect key comprehension strategies of prediction, visualization, connection, summarization, evaluation, and questioning. In other words, the student may be asked to take 2 minutes and respond to one of these:

- Describe the visualization you had while reading.
- What do you predict will happen next? Why?
- Did you connect personally to what you read, or did it connect to your world? Give examples.
- Write a 1-sentence summary of what you read today.
- What is your evaluation of what you read? Did you like it? Why?
- What questions do you want to ask the author?

An example of a Reading Log is in Resources for your consideration.

Scheduling Accountable Independent Reading

In self-contained, reading, or reading intervention classes, scheduling the 20 minutes for accountable independent reading is a given. The challenge is when students change classes or do not have a designated reading class.

All students who read below grade level should have accountable independent reading, and it is recommended for the other students as well. If the school has low reading achievement across all grades and the majority of students read below grade level, then a schoolwide accountable independent reading approach will support schoolwide improvement in reading. Lyman High School in Longwood, Florida, has the first 20 minutes of *each class period* designated as accountable independent reading time, resulting in reading comprehension scores that improve each year. Such schoolwide scheduling is important.

Other options are to have a rotation among the teacher team so that on Monday the language arts teacher schedules 20 minutes, on Tuesday the mathematics teacher schedules 20 minutes, and so on. This way, the responsibility for accountable independent reading is shared across the teachers. The bottom line is that if a school is committed to improving reading, then accountable independent reading will be nonnegotiable and supported by the school schedule, as well as with resources.

PRACTICAL TIPS FOR DEVELOPING FLUENCY

Tips for Reading and
Reading Intervention in Grades 4–12

- Students should read and reread important passages or especially books of their choice.
- Maximize the power of technology solutions to build fluency.
- Students read and reread, then record and listen to their reading.
- Provide unabridged audiobooks for students to have access to on-grade-level texts.
- Students should read 20 minutes each day with accountability.
- Provide fluent-reading models of a variety of texts.
- Encourage students to give book talks to other adults in the school.

Tips for English, Mathematics, Science, Social Studies, and Other Content Classes in Grades 4–12

- Encourage students to read high- interest newspaper or periodical selections near the independent reading level of the students. (Not for accountable independent reading.)
- Read orally to the students an essential paragraph in the text. Follow by asking students to read it chorally with you. Now ask them to read it silently for 30 seconds. Invite volunteers to read the essential passage orally. Ask students to tell you which of the words are essential vocabulary along with the meaning. Invite volunteers to share orally what the paragraph means.
- Students take 3 minutes and read essential text passages or a mathematics problem (selected by the teacher) to each other. Then students explain in their own words for 1 minute each what the passage or problem means. Last, take 1 more minute and have students ask their partner any question they have about the passage or problem. Unanswered questions should be offered to the entire class for explanation. If a mathematics problem is being read, students should work the problem and explain their answers.

(Continued)

(Continued)

- For homework, let students select an appropriate television program to watch, turning on the English closed caption. Students should have accountability for selected comprehension skills (main idea/details, literary elements, fact/opinion, cause/effect, sequence, comparison, contrast, inference, summary, etc.) or selected comprehension strategies (prediction and clarification, evaluation and evidence, connection, etc.).
- Provide a listening station in class that includes software or a DVD related to the content textbook or to another text related to the standards-based curriculum. Include comprehension accountability related to comprehension skills or comprehension strategies at the listening station.

Owning Comprehension Strategies

On-grade-level readers develop their own comprehension strategies for independent reading. Most of us became strategic readers on our own without direct instruction related to literacy strategies. Think about your own reading. Do you find reading certain types of print easier than others? Do you find yourself rereading when you encounter difficult text or perhaps skipping a sentence to see if you can understand the concept with further reading? What do you do while you read? Underline? Highlight? Write in the margins? Make a graphic of important information? Good readers use literacy strategies before they read, during their reading, and after their reading to heighten comprehension of the text.

Those who struggle to comprehend generally do not employ the literacy strategies that good readers do; they continue to move their eyes over print, not even expecting to comprehend as they turn the pages. These students do not adjust strategies for easier or harder text; they believe all text to be equally difficult. Teaching, modeling, and practicing the strategies that expert readers employ is the fourth nonnegotiable expectation of daily practice, which has the intent of assisting all readers to own the literacy strategies of expert readers. Owning the strategies, like owning vocabulary, comes after multiple opportunities to have the literacy strategies directly instructed, modeled, and practiced with the support of a teacher. Once students own strategies, they will use the strategies to monitor their comprehension.

Gains in reading comprehension occur when teachers *consistently* implement the nonnegotiables: In this case, teach, model, and practice the strategies of expert readers to move students from compliance to engagement. The previous four chapters focused on developing an understanding of the components of reading that are precursors of creating independent readers, writers, and content learners. In this chapter, we will focus on the ultimate goal for students in Grades 4 through 12 to become strategic in comprehending various types of text through consistent incorporation of before-, during-, and after-reading literacy strategies, resulting in higher engagement in learning.

KEY COMPREHENSION STRATEGIES

There are numerous literacy strategies a teacher can incorporate into instructional plans before, during, and after reading (Biancarosa & Snow, 2004; Wilson, 2004). For consistency, it is recommended that teachers select key strategies to begin the journey of teaching, modeling, and practicing with students. While teachers may be able to incorporate very complex strategies, keep in mind that the goal is to move ownership of strategies from the teacher to the students so they can be independent readers, writers, and content learners. As with any instruction, begin where the students are.

You are invited to consider the following seven strategies and graphic organizers for beginning the process of literacy strategy ownership with your students. These have been selected because they are research based, pull students upward regardless of reading level, and in combination form many of the more complex strategies (such as reciprocal teaching) that teachers may use in instruction. Also, they are effective with any grade level and any content area.

1. Prediction

2. Clarification

3. Asking and answering questions

4. Summarization

5. Visualization

6. Connection to self, other texts, and the world beyond school

7. Evaluation

Prediction

Probably the most commonly used literacy strategy is prediction before reading. When introducing a new book to be read by an entire class, teachers frequently ask students to predict what it may be about.

Before doing so, teachers are invited to directly instruct students where to find the clues or evidence to support a prediction so that predicting is not guessing. Where would we suggest students look for clues? Viewing the title, pictures, graphs, charts, headings, sidebars, and perhaps even footnotes would be good places to begin. Those who are more well-read will suggest looking at the author since authors tend to have genres, topics, or concepts that they favor for their writing. For instance, when I see a title by Paul Fleischman, I predict that the text will include either science or social studies concepts, be engaging to adolescents, and probably be written in two or more voices.

Of course, students read more than books in school. In fact, they read more chapters or handouts than entire books. Consider using the same prediction strategy when introducing any text—a chapter in the mathematics, social studies, health, or biology book, or yes, even a passage in a literature anthology. Preparing students to read these more difficult texts is often omitted, but it may be more essential for success than for the shared novel. Prediction is intended to access prior knowledge or build knowledge before scaffolding to the text.

Can prediction be used during or after reading? Most assuredly it can be. In fact, reading comprehension of text will be enhanced if teachers directly teach, model, and practice prediction during and after the reading. Do not get in a hurry and let the students off with guessing. Guessing is not prediction. When a student makes a prediction, ask, "Can you share your evidence?" or "On what are you basing that prediction?" When you expect evidence, you have raised the expectation of thinking and the level of comprehension. Keep in mind that the value of prediction is not in the correctness of the prediction, but the engagement of thinking that leads to the prediction.

Clarification

When we assist students in accessing prior knowledge before reading, we support them in clarifying information and any misconceptions that they may have learned in the past. However, this is not the key clarification time. During reading and after reading are the key clarification times for expert readers.

Clarification is a strategy that readers who lack comprehension do not have. Whatever they think the reading is about when they first encounter the text, they continue to think the same regardless of the words in print. For instance, if before reading, students make a prediction related to the upcoming reading, those who lack comprehension will continue to make the same prediction and never correct their faulty thinking. Expert readers monitor their comprehension and correct misconceptions, while poor readers do not. Directly teaching students that when we begin reading a chapter, article, or book and think it is about one thing but later can clarify that it is about something else or confirms the prediction empowers them to use the same strategy.

Mental Model: Prediction and Clarification

When browsing through a bookstore, I spotted a book called *Sacred Hoops* by Phil Jackson. After previewing the cover, I purchased the book because I believed it addressed ethical leadership. Once I began reading the book, which I enjoyed immensely and have recommended to others (evaluation), I realized that had I known the author, Phil Jackson, I could have more accurately predicted what the book was about. Yes, it was about leadership, but the context for me was unexpected: leadership in the context of building a team of National Basketball Association players! Someone more knowledgeable about professional sports would have predicted that the book would be about basketball but clarified when they read it that the text included leadership, team building, and ethics. Expert readers make the clarifications, and readers who lack comprehension do not.

Asking and Answering Questions

Most teachers would wonder why asking and answering questions is a literacy strategy. Next time you walk into a classroom, conduct a mini-classroom action research. Post this question for a quickwrite: "Whose responsibility is it to ask questions and why?" Follow with a brief sharing of student responses. You will find that more struggling students think it is the teacher's responsibility to ask questions and the student's responsibility to answer questions. There will probably be some students who realize that asking questions is characteristic of expert readers.

Classrooms that I visit frequently have the practice of students answering questions after reading, usually those found in the textbook. This common practice is why students think that asking questions is the teacher's job and answering the questions is their job. If answering questions in the textbook is what you would like students to do, as a before-reading literacy strategy, you may want to preview a few well-selected questions with the students prior to reading to focus their purpose for reading.

By directly teaching students to ask questions related to the reading or to question the author, you are assisting students in strategically comprehending. Students can generate questions before the reading, during reading,

Figure 5.1   Questioning and Clarification

I wonder?	Clarification	Page	Notes

and after reading. Asking students to question supports the concept of safe classrooms discussed in Chapter 1. Specific strategies will be offered in more detail in Chapter 6, Comprehending With Higher Levels of Thinking.

One technique for assisting students in getting started with questioning is to have them make a 2-column or 4-column log. "I wonder" would be the heading of the first column and "Clarification" would head the second column. If you want more thinking and evidence, add columns for the page number of the clarification and notes the reader may want to make. Figure 5.1 provides you with an idea for making this graphic organizer.

"I wonder" and "Clarification" would be completed during and after reading. These columns teach students that they should be thinking about the reading as their eyes pass over print, asking questions, and making clarifications. All "I wonders" will not have clarifications. That may come in class discussion afterward, or perhaps the student will need to investigate to learn further. Isn't this the goal to motivate students to learn more?

SUMMARIZATION

"Write a summary of what you just read, *and* remember to indent the first line; have a topic sentence, at least three supporting sentences, and a concluding sentence." This is a common application of summarization given to determine the level of comprehension of the reading. When I survey teachers to ask what percentage of their students are successful with this summarization, the response is low, always under 50%! Only the teacher pleasers and excellent students complete the assignment. This low percentage of success tells me that something in the process needs to change, because the only way to improve student achievement is to successfully engage more students more often.

Consider this as an alternative. "Write a one-sentence summary of what we have just read." Ask yourself, "What percent of my students will complete this task?" My experience is 99%–100% will! Now that you have all of the students engaged, you can develop the assignment further. Below-grade-level readers may have simple sentences, and better readers may have compound or complex sentences demonstrating that they have read and comprehended the passage. Teachers who try the one-sentence summary have provided feedback that indicates it works very well with the students and enhances comprehension.

Other alternatives to the general summary paragraph include the following:

- Identify 3 points to remember.
- Select the 4 most essential elements of the passage.
- What does the author want you to remember?
- What does the author believe to be important?
- Paraphrase the main idea and supporting details.

Notice that in each of these assignments, the student is not given a format, and the student cannot copy anything from the text. Students are asked to generate content first in their own words. You will want this phrase to become automatic in your classroom voice: "In your own words . . ." Determine what is important and what is not, then putting the information into sentences, and next into a paragraph. The strategy of summarization when used as described will enhance student writing, and you will be surprised that the amount of content in the writing will increase; no more content-free paragraphs.

Visualization

In contrast to the common usage of prediction and summarization, visualization is not typically employed. When you read a book, do you have pictures in your head? Which is better, the book you have read or the movie when you go see it? For most of us, the visualization of our reading is better than what we see in a theater. In contrast to expert readers, many below-grade-level readers do not have pictures in their heads when they read. Teaching, modeling, and practicing the literacy strategy of visualization will improve comprehension.

In Grades 4–12, there are teachers who mistakenly believe that allowing students to use drawings or visuals is babyish or demeaning to students. Far from insulting students, visualization honors them in a way that allows them to demonstrate understanding with alternative means. Visualization includes all of the senses: sight, smell, hearing, taste, and touch.

There are a number of ways to teach students to visualize. Read to them a short passage and ask them to jot down words that represent what they visualized. You do the same. Facilitate sharing of those key words and the commensurate pictures with the class. When below-grade-level readers hear the other students' visualizations, an expectation to visualize is created, and they learn from the modeling of others. When students read a passage, give them a choice of writing a one-sentence summary or sketching what was most important. Teachers should model the sketch. When teachers use stick figures and model that visualization is not necessarily artistic work but a representation of the reading, they will be willing to try. Examples of sketches of visualizations can be posted around the room to assist in the development of the print- and literacy-rich environment. This includes your visualization! Visualizations will often arise out of connections made to personal experience. These two strategies work well together.

In mathematics, students tend to have more difficulty with word problems than with computation. This mathematical achievement issue is related to comprehension, and visualization can help. As students read a word problem, ask them to sketch out what the problem is saying, adding the numbers. Some students may be able to do this in their heads, but those who need extra support will need to sketch on their paper.

Connections

Remembering is linking one piece of information to another. To learn new information we need to access prior knowledge and build on it. These are examples of making connections and are the basis for integrated curriculum. Connections assist students in understanding and making sense of various pieces of information. The literacy strategy of making connections moves learning from short-term memory to long-term memory so that it can be retrieved later. In other words, do you want your students to remember what they are learning later in life, or just until the test? If the purpose is for students to retain what they are learning beyond the test, then always use the literacy strategy of making connections either to self, to another text, or to the world beyond school.

Here are the kinds of questions that encourage making connections.

- Does this passage remind you of anything else that we have read?
- Have you ever had an experience like this?
- Have you ever felt like the character did in the book?
- Do you use geometry in your life? Do you know anyone who does?
- Where will you use algebra?
- Look around the room. How many right angles can you identify? Write them down.
- We have just read about Wilma Rudolph. Do you know anyone who has overcome any kind of adversity?
- How does a student's life in the Middle East compare to your life?

Making connections also assists with developing motivation to do the work. The ease of making connections in certain books is why authors such as Kate DiCamillo, Gary Paulson, Gary Soto, Sandra Cisneros, and Sharon Draper are so popular with students. When students do not see a purpose, relevance, or personal application, they tend not to do their best. In standards-based curriculum classes, working to be sure students are making connections will motivate their learning and move it to long-term memory.

Evaluation

The last of the seven key literacy strategies that is recommended for you to teach, model, and practice until students own them is evaluation. Again, good readers form opinions about their reading and can support those opinions in contrast to below-grade-level readers who do not read with evaluation in mind. Evaluation is an easy literacy strategy to incorporate before, during, and after reading. Used properly, evaluation will require supporting statements and evidence.

When previewing the text before reading, check with the students to see if they think they will enjoy the passage. Why or why not? During the reading of a shared novel, ask students how many read ahead. Why did they read ahead—because they want to find out what happened? Were you immediately drawn in or did it take a while? After reading, would you recommend the book to a friend? Would you reread it independently? Was your interest developed when we read about the Civil War to the point that you will personally read more about it?

Evaluation should not be taught as, "Did you like the passage/book? Yes or no?" Try to develop questions that require an extended response or short answer with support either from the reading or from connections made to self, other text, or to the world. An example would be, "Bird flu is of concern to many people. Evaluate how effective the author is in presenting tips for avoiding this illness." A mathematical application would be, "We have learned two different strategies for solving this type of geometry problem. Which of the strategies do you think is easier and why?" Practicing extended responses and short answers within the context of daily instruction will support students when they encounter them on standardized assessments.

TEACHING STRATEGIES WITH SCAFFOLDING

Consider teaching, modeling, and practicing each of the seven strategies one at a time with your students when reading text. Gradually, use more than one at a time until the students seem to own them. Then, rather than offering a strategy, ask the students, "Which of the seven key literacy strategies would be helpful?" or "Which did you use?" or "Select one of the seven key literacy strategies to show me you're thinking about the reading." A good idea is to have students make a poster to remind them of the seven key strategies and have it visible in your print- and literacy-rich classroom.

Although the discussion in this chapter has focused on teaching, modeling, and practicing literacy strategies of expert readers, these strategies are supportive of all students reading and writing at a higher level. Teachers of "honors" and "advanced placement" classes whose students read on and above grade level find the strategies helpful because the texts their students are reading are often more than two grade levels above the student and may be on college level. You will find these strategies in research-based texts for below-grade-level readers, like *Read XL* (Scholastic) or *SourceBook* (Great Source) and in texts for on-grade-level and above-grade-level readers, like *SpringBoard* from the College Board.

In Figure 5.2 you can see the relationship of the key strategies to levels of thinking (Bloom et al., 1956). By using these strategies, the student is working at higher levels of thinking, hence developing deeper levels of understanding.

For those who would like to study literacy strategies in more depth, there are many resources available. Those that follow are teacher-friendly and are excellent resources for individual teachers and for study groups.

Allen, J. (2004). *Tools for teaching content literacy.* Portland, ME: Stenhouse Publishers.

Beers, K. (2003). *When kids can't read: What teachers can do.* Portsmouth, NH: Heinemann.

Barton, M. L., & Heidman, C. (2002). *Teaching reading in mathematics* (2nd ed.). Aurora, CO: McREL.

Barton, M. L., & Jordan, D. L. (2001). *Teaching reading in science.* Aurora, CO: McREL.

Billmeyer, R., & Barton, M. L. (1998). *Teaching reading in the content areas: If not me, then who?* Aurora, CO: McREL.

Daniels, H., & Zimmerman, S. (2004). *Subjects matter.* Portsmouth, NH: Heinemann.

Robb, L. (2000). *Teaching reading in middle school.* New York: Scholastic, Inc.

Stephens, E. C., & Brown, J. E. (2000). *A handbook of content literacy strategies: 75 practical reading and writing ideas.* Norwood, MA: Christopher-Gordon Publishers.

Figure 5.2   Relationship of Literacy Strategies to Levels of Thinking

	Knowledge	Comprehension	Application	Analysis	Synthesis	Evaluation
Prediction				X		
Summarization		X			(1 sentence) X	
Clarification				X		
Visualization			X			
Questioning				X		
Connection			X			
Evaluation						X

TO WHAT EXTENT SHOULD STRATEGIES BE INCORPORATED?

As a nonnegotiable expectation of daily practice, teaching, modeling, and practicing strategies of expert readers, it is recommended that all print instruction be framed with before-reading, during-reading, and after-reading strategies. Equalizing use of strategies in these three components of an instructional plan will enhance comprehension, particularly of a student who reads below grade level.

Mental Model: Fourth-Grade Small Group

When observing a small-group session of fourth-grade below-grade-level readers, I noticed that the teacher was explicit with strategies before, during, and after reading. Students had on the table in front of them *Escape North: The Story of Harriet Tubman.* She read the title to the students and asked them if they had heard of Harriet Tubman. Students offered information they thought they knew. In social studies, they had learned about the Underground Railroad and how it related to slavery. Underground Railroad was clarified: "It is really not underground, but secret." Next, the teacher asked the students to look at the cover and the illustrations to see what they could learn from them. Students were eager and offered ideas they thought they saw, making predictions of what they would read. One student saw a picture of Harriet Tubman in the back of the book and exclaimed, "Look, here is her picture! She lived to be 92 years old!" After previewing the text, the teacher read the first chapter of the book to the students as they followed along. She paused, checking for understanding along the way. Upon completion of the first chapter, students were asked a few questions to ensure comprehension. Then they were asked to read the second chapter independently. Following the reading of the second chapter, the teacher guided the students in making a story map of this biography, completing the day's small-group session.

Teachers should keep in mind that for a student to read a text independently, he or she must know about 95% of the vocabulary. However, with teacher support using before-, during-, and after-reading strategies, a student can comprehend text even though he or she knows only about 75% of the words (Beers, 2003). Framing instruction this way gives access to on-grade-level content that a student cannot access independently or to above-grade-level content that the on-grade-level reader is challenged with.

The time invested and the degree to which a teacher incorporates strategies depends on the complexity of the text and the difficulty for the unique group of students. When below-grade-level readers are given a passage to read on their reading levels, not as much support is needed as when they are given an on-grade-level passage. In contrast, when teaching a heterogeneous group of physical science students, the teacher may be careful to frame instruction with literacy strategies to be sure to support all students. In other words, sometimes you use few strategies for easily understood text, and sometimes you spend a lot of time preparing students to read, supporting them during the reading and supporting comprehension after reading.

SMART TASKS

One of the challenges today is engaging the entire class with any assignment. It seems that if the teacher finds an assignment that everyone can engage in. it is too easy for many. This is why teachers often shoot for the middle of the group; that is, they teach on-grade-level concepts with instructional strategies that overwhelm many students and yet bore others. SMART Tasks is an application of literacy strategies and appears to be one of the answers to the challenge of engaging all students in a heterogeneous classroom.

SMART Tasks are those that are:

- Specific
- Measurable
- Action oriented
- Results driven
- Time limited

Think about a time when you assigned a task and it had multiple steps. How many students skipped or forgot a step? How many put their heads down or pretended to do the work? SMART Tasks are rigorous, probably multistep assignments that have undergone a task analysis to determine the individual steps required for successful completion. By analyzing a rigorous assignment and breaking the steps down into specific, measurable, action-oriented, and results-driven components, then limiting the time that students have to complete the task, it becomes SMART. As a result of high engagement and fast pace, completion rate goes up. Students do not get overwhelmed with multisteps because the task is given in small steps that engage all learners—where they are. The tasks are measurable, require action, and gets results quickly so that checking for understanding and then providing correctives happen immediately for the students. With limited time, students cannot get off task, which is one of the major causes of disruptive behavior, particularly with older students.

Here is an example that I frequently employ. Read aloud to students or ask them to read a passage and then write a one-sentence summary. When a one-sentence summary is assigned, the lowest reader/writer will attempt the task and the most advanced reader/writer is forced not to regurgitate the information in its entirety (as they have been conditioned to do) but to synthesize and to operate at a higher level. If the teacher says, "Write a summary," or "Write a paragraph," struggling students may not engage at all, and not even pick up their pencils. Following the one-sentence summary writing, I always have students share what they have written, providing an invitation for success for all students. Any incorrect information in the one-sentence summaries is open to the other students to provide evidence to encourage correction. Then students are given, say, two minutes to add to their sentence or write another one with the information they have heard from their peers. After writing several one-sentence summaries, ask students to create a paragraph out of the sentences they have created. Higher-performing students resist SMART Tasks but will engage in the activity, lower-performing students will engage in the activity, and then you have overall higher engagement on higher-level tasks by the entire spectrum of readers.

Mental Model: SMART Tasks in Special Education

Recently, a teacher of students with disabilities relayed to me her experience using SMART Tasks. The first of October she introduced the text *Seedfolks* (Fleischman, 1997) to her small class and read the first chapter, "Kim," to them and then asked the students to write a one-sentence summary. Her student reading at the lowest level wrote, "It was about a girl." This was the first written work the 14-year-old had done so far in the school year. Because she was successful, she continued to try to do other assignments as they were given. In contrast, the highest reader wrote a complex sentence with supporting details after the same read-aloud. In other words, students began with a small doable task, and using all the processes of literacy, continued to build to rigor through multiple drafts. The lowest-performing student engaged in the learning, and the highest-performing student was challenged to think and operate at a higher level.

GRAPHIC ORGANIZERS

In addition to literacy strategies, graphic organizers assist in comprehension of various texts, particularly nonfiction and expository text. Keep in mind that as students reach the middle grades, they are measured predominately with nonfiction and expository text. Graphic organizers are nonlinguistic representations, useful in making concrete the abstract concepts of the printed word. Bubble maps and other charts assist students in seeing relationships among characters, concepts, and vocabulary. Sequence charts, story boards, and flowcharts show chronology and relationships. Venn diagrams are excellent for comparing and contrasting two concepts or elements. KWL (What do you know? What do you want to know? What have you learned?) incorporates before- and after-reading strategies. For high school students, it is suggested that you adjust KWL to be KNL, changing What do you want to know? to What do you need to learn? Think about KNLS, with the S being What do you still need to learn?

Be sure to work with the students in completing graphic organizers, discuss the content, and scaffold to writing from the graphic organizers. These steps will prevent the graphic organizers from becoming worksheets and maintain their integrity as supports for thinking about the reading and writing. Graphic organizers are bridges between the text, reading comprehension, and writing.

Mental Model: FANG

John Wright, principal of Timber Creek High School, worked with his school's literacy council to include an expectation of consistency in their fail-safe literacy system. The literacy council chose to develop one graphic organizer to be used by every teacher in all grade levels and content areas in the school at least once a month. It is called FANG, which relates to the school mascot, the wolf. Some laughingly suggest it means "take a bite out of reading."

When you look at Figure 5.3 FANG, Timber Creek High School, note that it frames instruction with before, during, and after reading. Which of the key strategies do you see in FANG? Does it focus on low or high levels of thinking?

Figure 5.3   FANG, Timber Creek High School

Before Reading Questions to Guide My Reading (3 questions to answer during reading)	**During Reading** Word Collection (Words I don't know)
During Reading Annotate the article (Things to remember)	**Author's Purpose** (Why did the author write this?)
After Reading Main Idea/Thesis in Author's Words (1 sentence from the reading)	**Supporting Evidence** (3 points to support the main idea)
Synthesis (Connect the article to you, another text, or the world)	**One-Sentence Summary** (Summarize in your own words)

SOURCE: Used with permission of Timber Creek High School.

Prior to implementation, the literacy council provided teachers with professional development on FANG with modeling and examples from each of the content areas. They were told that using FANG does not mean to use all eight of the cells each time. A teacher can select the ones most applicable to the reading or all eight if that is useful. Although FANG was at first required periodically, teachers soon realized that it assisted them in organizing their instruction and resulted in greater comprehension. On visiting classrooms on non-FANG days, I observed teachers using the graphic organizer and students engaged with the process. You are encouraged to purposefully and strategically develop your own graphic organizers that reflect the key literacy strategies and higher levels of thinking.

Text Structure

In addition to comprehension strategies and graphic organizers, understanding the structure of a text is helpful. Text structure seems obvious to those of us who are good readers. Until Grade 4, most of what students have read is fiction, but now the majority becomes nonfiction and teaching text structure becomes very important. In Chapter 1, texts were discussed but are briefly included here since understanding text structure supports developing comprehension. Below-grade-level readers do not understand the parameters of how textbooks and other print are organized, particularly content textbooks, nonfiction, and expository text. Remember, you have a teacher's guide and perhaps have attended professional development on how to effectively use the textbook. All but the best students are naive to the textbook's organization. Point out to them where to find important information. What do the highlighted, boldfaced, italicized, or underlined words mean? What are text boxes for? What should you read first and last?

Teachers interested in resources for assisting content teachers with the direct teaching of text structure may find the companion to the *Reader's Handbook*, titled *Content Area Guides*, for language arts, mathematics, social studies, and science helpful. These content area guides explicitly teach the text structure, how to use textbooks, and how to teach strategies within each of these content areas to enhance comprehension.

Mental Model: Review in Law Studies

On a recent visit to a law studies class, the students were reviewing for the end-of-unit exam. Rather than observing disengagement with study sheets and lecture reviews, I observed 100% engagement on the part of students whose reading levels varied from above- to below-grade-level readers.

Upon entering the class, I noted that students had their desks turned in clusters of 3 or 4 and that the students were in discussion. Each student cluster had been given a section of the textbook for which it was responsible to review for the class. Rather than a general review, each cluster was to write a one-sentence summary (main idea) of the section and three supporting details. The one-sentence summary was written on a sentence strip and posted on the whiteboard in the front of the classroom. The three supporting details were then written on the whiteboard by the students. "Freedom" was written in the center of the whiteboard around which the students added their cluster's thinking. When the work was completed, each cluster came to the front of the room and orally provided additional insight for the remainder of the class.

As you read the vignette, which of the nonnegotiables and exemplary literacy practices did you think about? Here are the ones I observed.

- All literacy processes: reading, writing, listening, speaking, viewing, thinking, communication through multiple-symbol systems
- Chunking
- Differentiated instruction: small groups
- After reading: one-sentence summary and three details
- Visual support: graphic organizer
- Label of reading assessment skill: main idea, supporting details, paraphrasing

This exemplary instructional plan could be applied to any content area either as an introduction to a chapter or as a review. It ensures that all students have equal access to on-grade-level content curriculum while improving reading, writing, and content learning.

Mental Model: Literature

Students opened their anthologies to the designated selection. The teacher instructed them to get out their sticky notes and pens. After preparing the students to read, the teacher turned on the companion compact disc of the selection. As students followed along in their text, they wrote notes on the sticky notes and stuck them to the passage. After 1–2 minutes, the teacher stopped the compact disc, asked questions, and asked students to share their sticky notes. Then she continued repeating the same strategy over and over again. At the end of the reading, she asked the students to put their names on the sticky notes, took them up, and gave them credit for note taking.

What is particularly interesting in this case is that on an earlier visit, the teacher had shared that she was having difficulty engaging the students with the reading and that their note taking was meager and unacceptable. After coaching her to consider letting students use sticky notes to take notes right on the text (which are far less intimidating than notebook paper), she decided to try it. What she learned was that all of the students liked writing on the sticky notes and are taking notes. Their participation in class has improved, reducing her discipline problems, and student grades have improved. This teacher made standards-based curriculum accessible to students by structuring her print instruction with strategies and tools that she herself had used.

PRACTICAL TIPS FOR OWNING COMPREHENSION STRATEGIES

Tips for Reading, Reading Intervention, English, and Language Arts in Grades 4–12

- Focus on content comprehension first; then ask students to write in the form you require.
- Post helping strategies for student to refer to when they find they are not comprehending:

  Reread.

  Skip and see if it makes sense.

  Try a popper! (substitute another word)

  Read the introduction, summary.

  Read the questions at the end.

  Out-to-the-side number sequences.

  Highlight.

Tips for Content Classes in Grades 4–12

- Assign a 2-minute quick write (to access prior knowledge). Now share what you have written.
- Three points to remember: Individually or in groups of no more than four students, read and determine the most important information in a passage. Then they should share with the class by posting their answers, then orally sharing. Following, each student should individually edit his/her 3 points to remember, which may mean that there are more than 3 and that details have been added.
- Chunking: Divide a section of the textbook or nonfiction passage into sections and then assign a section to groups within

---

(Continued)

(Continued)

the class. After a specific time for reading the section, the groups will select important information to post and then share it orally with the class. Essentially, the entire class will end up with an outline of the entire text to use as a guide for rereading and initially reading the remainder of the text. All students have access by limiting their initial volume of reading until after listening, speaking, viewing, and thinking related to the text.

- Assign homework only for extended independent practice after directly teaching, modeling, and guiding practice in class. Homework must reinforce correct learning, not incorrect learning. In other words, if students practice incorrectly, it will be very difficult to unlearn. Practice makes permanent.
- Read a mathematics problem to the class with them following along. Ask the class to note on their paper what information is essential to understanding the problem. (You may want to use a graphic organizer that shows the problem, essential information, definitions of key words, sketch space, and problem-solving space.) Invite volunteers to raise their hands, and keep encouraging hands to go up until at least half the class is raising them. Call on one of the last ones to share essential information or call on another student to share. Ask the class to raise their hands indicating that they agree with the student or disagree with the student. Students then would be called on to explain their agreement or disagreement. The teacher may continue to work through the problem-solving process (Step one: Read and understand the problem) until she is confident that all students comprehend the problem and are ready to attempt finding the solution. After finding the solution, say, "Explain your answer."
- Use sticky notes and sticky pointers to mark important information and to note questions students have about the reading.
- With sticky notes, write notes in the margins (Remember this! Important. Ask the teacher.)
- Give one set of directions. After students complete that task, give the second set of directions.
- Use strategies to ensure comprehension before moving to comprehension skill questions (cause and effect, author's purpose, sequence, compare, contrast, making differences, drawing conclusions, main idea, supporting details).

Comprehending With Higher Levels of Thinking

Facilitating the reading, writing, and content learning of students in Grades 4–12 is more complex than it may first appear. As discussed in Chapters 1–5, students need to be able decode, acquire vocabulary, and comprehend various types of texts independently. To accomplish this complex charge, you have been offered fail-safe literacy as a system. The purpose of fail-safe literacy is to create a systematic instructional planning process that will ensure more proficient readers, writers, and content learners. In this chapter, those concepts are connected to higher levels of thinking.

HIGHER LEVELS OF THINKING

While writing this book, I received an e-mail from a high school principal who is known to be an instructional leader. The first 9-week grading period had ended with all teachers giving a 9-week exam. As a step in monitoring instruction, the principal scanned the exams that had been given and noted that only in a few Advanced Placement classes were any exam questions higher than factual or comprehension, the two lowest levels of thinking. Knowing that this level of work would not advance student achievement as measured on the state assessment, she began facilitating higher levels of thinking in daily classroom practice.

The experience of this principal is common. The majority of teachers and textbooks focus on knowledge (recall) and comprehension (retell, summarize, or compare and contrast within the text) in contrast to application, analysis, synthesis, and evaluation. Chapter 5 includes Figure 5.3, which shows the relationship of literacy strategies to levels of thinking. This chapter offers more ideas for aligning classroom practice with higher levels of thinking.

When scaffolding from low levels of thinking to high levels of thinking, these terms are used in ascending order: knowledge-comprehension-application-analysis-synthesis-evaluation (Bloom, et al., 1956). For effective learning to take place, some educators have mistakenly assumed that learners must start at the bottom of the levels of thinking and work their way "up." For instance, if we start with a knowledge level such as main idea, and the students cannot get the main idea, then some teachers would not move on to summarization, or higher levels of thinking. In contrast, the fail-safe literacy approach is to ask all levels of questions every day.

The problem encountered with this inference is that each subsequent "level" does not self-propel into the next. There is no instinctive transition. It also follows that comprehension does not automatically connect to application. It is this lack of direct inductive connection from lower to higher in levels of thinking that causes great difficulty. Teachers will typically wonder how they can get their students to the higher-order thinking skills when the most struggling students may not have mastered the knowledge and comprehension levels.

One place to begin with instruction utilizing higher levels of thinking is with the literacy processes. Figure 6.1 offers ideas for incorporating higher levels of thinking using these processes. When using various levels of thinking with students, teachers should label what they are doing. "Now, I'm going to ask you an analysis question. You will have to think about it before answering." Teachers may want to use this resource when making instructional plans to ensure incorporation of all levels of thinking every day.

QUESTIONING STRATEGIES

Engaging students in higher levels of thinking is critical for improving performance on standardized assessments. This is true whether the assessments are required by the state or are the Scholastic Aptitude Test or Advanced Placement Tests. As we have discussed, one approach is to be sure to use all levels of thinking (Bloom, et al., 1956) each day in instruction and in the questions you ask.

Some states have turned to Webb's Depth of Knowledge for developing assessment items. If that is the case in your state, you may want to learn a little more about the system of question development.

Figure 6.1   Literacy Processes and Levels of Thinking

Examples	Literacy Processes					
	Reading	Writing	Listening	Speaking	Viewing	Thinking
Levels of Thinking						
Evaluation	Relate meaning beyond school and student's life.	Critique with supporting evidence. Put in priority order.	Discriminate between ideas. Agree or disagree?	Articulate to an audience relationships among varying points of view.	Identify and explain nuances in a presentation, CD, or visual.	Discern important and unimportant information and the value of each.
Synthesis	Distill deeper meaning.	1-sentence summary.	Understand and summarize.	Speak knowledgeably about a topic.	Interpret the meaning of the visual.	Combine new knowledge with old knowledge.
Analysis	Relate to other texts. Predict with evidence.	Compare and contrast ideas with another author/text.	Use a rubric to compare various speakers.	Share relationship to other texts.	Assign value to the visual on a rubric.	Develop scale of understanding.
Application	Connect or relate to student's life or text.	Connect or relate to another setting, person, or event.	While listening, visualize another setting.	Explain relationship to your life.	Use information in another way.	Transfer concept to another application.
Comprehension	Understand theme. Summarize.	Support with details or description.	Understand main idea.	Articulate supporting details or evidence.	Determine key points to remember.	Understand and explain.
Knowledge	Answers are right there: Who? What? When? Where? Why?	Sequence, main idea, cause/effect.	Retell story. Time line. Memorize facts.	Answer factually.	Understand key points.	Provide hierarchy, chronological order.

Another approach that teachers and students find realistic for implementation is Question-Answer Relationships or QAR. QAR is a research-based questioning strategy that ensures regular asking and answering of questions at all levels (Billmeyer & Barton, 1998). Both QAR and Webb's Depth of Knowledge are based on the levels of thinking developed by Bloom and his colleagues.

QAR 4 Levels of Questions

Level 1: Right There!

Answer is found in one place in the text.
Who? What? When? Where? How? List.

Level 2: Think & Search!

Answer is found in more than one place in the text.
Summarize. Compare. Contrast. What caused? Retell.
Explain. Find 2 examples. For what reason?

Level 3: Author & You!

Answer is not in the text, but you must read the
text and apply what you read.

Level 4: On My Own!

Questions are answered with information you have read
from the text and/or from other places. You must think to answer it.

There are four steps for implementing QAR. These steps should be implemented over time, gradually releasing the responsibility for generating the 4 levels of questions to the students.

Step 1. The teacher becomes an expert at asking the 4 levels of questions.

Step 2. The teacher directly teaches, models, and practices the 4 levels of questions with students.

Step 3. Students become expert at labeling the 4 levels of questions and answering them.

Step 4. Students ask the 4 levels of questions and answer them.

From these four steps it can be seen that the purpose, like all literacy strategies, is to create strategic expertise on the part of the students. In doing so, the work is shifted from the teacher to the students for generating the questions. If students can generate the 4 levels of questions, they can also answer them.

Teachers find advantages in using QAR over trying to use higher levels of questions with individual students. Here is what they tell me.

- QAR accomplishes the same thing but is simpler to use.
- QAR helps students know where to find the answers.
- QAR helps students comprehend what they are reading.
- QAR gives students a purpose for reading.
- QAR helps students monitor comprehension.
- QAR encourages higher-level thinking.
- QAR helps students to know that all questions are not answered by looking in the text.

MORE QUESTIONING TECHNIQUES

Expertise in questioning separates good teachers from great teachers. If you use QAR or any higher-level thinking strategy and have misconceptions or lack of expertise related to questioning, the purpose will not be achieved. Therefore, this section offers you ideas for becoming a role model for asking questions and engaging students while doing so. When you have the opportunity to observe teachers whose students make great gains, pay particular attention to their questioning techniques. Watch for these kinds of things.

- Calling on all students, rather than just a few
- Dignifying responses
- Providing wait and think time
- Probing
- Clarifying
- Engaging students

Teachers who are role models are consciously aware that they must engage all students. Those who are engaged believe they are liked by the teacher, which in itself is a motivator. To create higher levels of engagement with questioning, find a system that ensures you call on all students. Novice teachers tend to call on the teacher pleasers—those who everyone knows have the answers and whose hands fly into the air before the question is even out of the teacher's mouth!

Research on wait time is consistently supportive of higher student achievement (Good, 1982; Good & Brophy, 1994; Rowe, 1986). To engage more students with questions, ask the question and wait. Waiting provides think time. Thinking does not happen instantaneously. A more thoughtful answer is better than the fastest answer. Tell the students your strategy for asking questions. "When I ask questions, I will wait thirty seconds for you to think about the answer. Raise your hand when you have an answer." Be sure to call on students, regardless of when they raise their hands. If you consistently call on the first hand raised, you can be sure you will not get many hands raised. Or if students do raise their hands, they may do it expecting that you will call on the first person who raised his hand, who may not even have a response formulated.

Never call the name of the student and then ask the question. This is the most common questioning practice that I observe in classrooms of all grades and content areas. It disengages all students but the one whose name was called.

When waiting, if I do not get many hands in the air, I will become the auctioneer—"I have two hands, can I get three? Four? Now I have six, can I get seven? Yes! I have eight!" Then I may call on the one that has not contributed much that day. This technique energizes the room, students like it, and they know that I will continue until we have engagement. When using this strategy, I often will turn to a student whose hand is not up and ask, "Tawanda, do I see your hand going up?" If she responds affirmatively, then she answers. If she responds negatively, then I'll invite her to call on a student whose hand is up.

It may be difficult to keep up with which students have been called on and which ones have not. There are many techniques for supporting this important data. Many teachers maintain this information in their grade book with a dot or check next to the student's name on the given date. Other colleagues have accomplished the same objective with making their notes on the seating chart. Some teachers like to have each student's name on a 3 × 5 card and note the dates of correct answers. Some teachers call out questions, shuffle the cards, and then call on the student whose card is on top or the bottom.

The most important thing is to hold each student accountable and maintain a record of it. Students in Grades 4–12 will make a little more effort if grades are affected, so including class participation in a quantifiable way may work.

What can a teacher do when a student says, "I do not know"? Consider offering the option of passing or calling on another student. Either way, I would later return to the student who did not have an answer. The purpose is for all students to know they count equally in the classroom, because they will always be held accountable and be dignified.

When you call on students, they sometimes offer an incorrect answer. With a strong community of learners in place, both the students and teacher will honor the respondent. A technique to employ is, "How many agree with Jason's answer?" and "How many disagree with his answer?" Ask for support of each. Then, I suggest, return to Jason and ask, "What is your answer now?" This particular technique dignifies an incorrect response, makes sure that the student learns the correct response, and never lets a student off the hook. Holding students accountable means that they remain engaged and will remember the question and the answer.

Asking for agreement and disagreement and supporting evidence or thinking is excellent for moving levels of thinking up to application, analysis, and evaluation. Role-model teachers probe and ask for the thinking behind the thinking. They will listen carefully to what students say, and then add something like, "I'm not sure I fully understand what you are suggesting. Can you tell me a little more about _____?" or "I need some help in understanding what you are saying. Can you give me a specific example?" Regularly, probe and get students to further explain their answers this way. Students are used to teachers letting them off the hook with generalized answers rather than specific ones. When I first use this technique with students, they think they are incorrect so I have to be explicit and tell them that I will be probing. I will be asking for detail, and it does NOT mean that what they have said is wrong. It means that I am interested in their thinking! For many students, this type of teaching and questioning is a new experience. In the long run, they appreciate it, and engagement increases.

HIGHER THINKING WITH GRAPHIC ORGANIZERS

As we discussed in Chapter 5, graphic organizers are excellent for assisting students in organizing their thinking and scaffolding to writing about their thinking. When considering graphic organizers, think about how to leverage them to scaffold the student to higher levels of thinking. FANG, mentioned in Chapter 5, is an excellent example as it includes synthesis and points to remember.

Another graphic organizer to consider is an anticipation guide. Anticipation guides are used before reading to access prior knowledge and to predict (anticipate) the content in the reading. The teacher identifies five or six key comprehension points in the reading and writes them in statements, some true and some not true. Students read each statement prior to reading the text and indicate if they agree or disagree with each of the statements. During or after the reading, students return to the statements and indicate what the author said about the statements.

Scaffolding anticipation guides to higher levels of thinking can be done in two ways. The first is to modify the anticipation guide by adding a column for evidence and notes. Second, the items themselves can be on higher levels of thinking. For instance, if you use QAR, include items from levels 1–4.

Figure 6.2 Anticipation Guide

Before Reading Reader Agree/Disagree	Statement	During/After Reading Author Agree/Disagree
	Always call the student's name, then ask a question.	
	Ask high levels of questions even if students do not get the main idea.	
	Call only on students who raise their hands.	
	Summarizing is a high-level thinking assignment.	
	Expertise in questioning distinguishes good teachers from role-model teachers.	

Figure 6.3 Higher-Thinking Anticipation Guide

Before Reading Reader Agree/Disagree	Statement	During/After Reading Author Agree/Disagree	Evidence	Notes
	Call the student's name first, then ask the question.			
	Call only on students who raise their hands.			
	Never embarrass a student who is without an answer.			
	Teach students your questioning technique.			
	Considering the students' developmental stage is not important.			

Mental Model: Wilma Rudolph

Let me offer another example of scaffolding graphic organizers up in the levels of thinking. An excellent type of graphic organizer to use when students are describing a character or themselves is a character map. Without a character map, students may write boring descriptions of physical attributes like height, weight, and hair color. Scaffolding character maps up by having categories such as hopes, dreams, aspirations, fears, and disappointments gives greater insight into the character and will result in better discussion and writing. If the teacher is working on figures of speech, she may want to include categories such as thinks, smells, hears, and feels. Ask the students to have two entries for each category: one literal and one figurative. You may even want to add a third task, to provide evidence for the character traits they identify.

After reading *Wilma Unlimited: How Wilma Rudolph Became the Fastest Woman in the World* (Krull, 1996), students have written phrases like the following:

- She smells sweat, and she smells success.
- She smells after running, and she smells victory.
- She feels pain in her leg and feels resentment that she can walk.
- She feels happy that she plays basketball and feels unhappy that she cannot go to school.
- She thinks, "My leg hurts," and "I know I can."
- She loves her family and loves her faith.

These are examples of how to scaffold from low levels of thinking to higher levels of thinking while improving the students' use of language. The result will be better readers, writers, and content learners.

ALIGN INSTRUCTIONAL RESOURCES

In Chapter 5, the reader was invited to think about instructional resources and their alignment with before-reading, during-reading, and after-reading use of literacy strategies. Now think about the instructional resources that you have available related to levels of thinking. Do they include higher levels of thinking in the suggested assignments and questions, or do they focus on knowledge and comprehension? Look for resources that have built in all levels of thinking.

How can this evaluation be made quickly? Look at the objectives of a chapter. Do they focus on low-level, inert knowledge, or do they focus on students' developing and applying knowledge? Then look at the questions at the end of the chapter. Label these questions with either the levels of thinking or QAR levels of questions. All of the levels should be included if the text is going to assist you in facilitating higher levels of student performance on standardized assessment. The last suggestion for this evaluation is to look in the teacher's guide. Are the higher levels of thinking and questioning included there? In most cases, the higher levels are indicated to be optional for enrichment or for higher-performing students. In reality, these assignments are excellent for all students. Unfortunately, with the pressure teachers feel to "cover" content, these higher-level learning experiences and questions are often omitted. This omission results in more surface coverage, less depth of coverage with the assessment performance, and often less than proficient or not making adequate yearly progress (AYP).

Enhancing performance on standardized assessments with alignment of classroom practice includes levels of thinking, levels of questions, and types of texts read. What is the percentage of nonfiction versus fiction items in the reading-comprehension section of your assessment? In elementary schools, it is generally about 50%, in middle schools about 60%, and in high schools about 70%. How does this percentage relate to reading in school? If students read mostly fiction in school or are modeled the joy of reading fiction in school but are assessed with a majority of nonfiction, we have misalignment of instructional experience. My observation in intervention or regular classes is that teachers attempt to correct this misalignment with test-preparation passages that are nonfiction and are followed by multiple-choice questions and a few extended-response questions.

There are issues to reflect on with this approach. First of all, students find many test-preparation resources to be boring and uninteresting. Second, these resources tend to be disconnected from the standards-based content curriculum, although they are connected to reading skills measured on standardized assessments. And last, few of these passages have items representing higher levels of thinking. While these test-preparation materials may assist with understanding the format of assessment, they will not assist students in becoming better readers, nor will they create joy in reading nonfiction but may actually discourage it. In contrast, materials that we have mentioned previously, such as *Read XL* and *SourceBook*, are predominately nonfiction and support preparation for assessment. Classroom magazines like *Time for Kids, Scope, UpFront, Science World, Junior Scholastic,* and *Action* serve the same purpose and are particularly engaging to students.

Teacher guides for these resources support both science and social studies standards-based curriculum and literacy learning. On December 17, 2004, www.Timeforkids.com included standard features of *Time for Kids*. Power Words (vocabulary) were included, such as *probe*. Under Nonfiction Literacy Strategies, the Making Connections feature suggested, "Challenge the students to identify events with the cover. What makes a news event important?" The Making Connections feature is explicitly one of the seven key literacy strategies, and this particular one incorporates the literacy processes of viewing and thinking, then scaffolds to a QAR level 4 question (on my own). Another feature is Critical Thinking. This particular issue asks, "What people, places, or events will still be in the news in 2005? Why do you think the editors chose these stories? What additional events would you have chosen?" These are excellent examples of standards-based supplementary resources aligned with the fail-safe belief about literacy and high levels of thinking.

Mental Model: Align Classroom Resources

In *Junior Scholastic*, the majority of entries are nonfiction. In the April 11, 2003, issue, six out of the seven are nonfiction, including maps, graphs, and charts with comprehension questions. The seventh is a play based on Henry VIII, which teaches history. These entries all are developmentally appropriate and engaging, and they enhance reading and content learning.

This periodical has a blocked section for many articles called, Your Turn: Think About It. The April 11, 2003, issue of *Junior Scholastic* has this example. "What is it like to have a member of your family serving in the U.S. military in Iraq?" (p. 11). What level of question is this? To scaffold to learning more, the question is followed with, "Read about U.S. teens whose relatives are stationed in the Gulf: www.scholastic.com/militarykids" (p. 11). Here is another entry in that issue. "What do you think can be done to promote greater understanding of Arab Americans?" (p. 13). What level of question is this one?

Mental Model: Test-Preparation Resources

In the autumn, I was visiting an intensive reading intervention classroom. When I arrived, I was quite impressed with the level of engagement of the students. They were in groups of four and were reading a nonfiction passage about two popular female vocalists in a test-preparation workbook. Clearly, the characters in the passage were of interest to them, and they had adequate background knowledge to comprehend the passage. After reading, the groups were to make a chart comparing and contrasting the two vocalists. Comparison and contrast are comprehension skills found on most assessments that often challenge students.

In debriefing with the teacher, we discussed the positives of the learning experience and how she could scaffold the same instruction to be more effective. First of all, having students interested in reading nonfiction is excellent. Practicing compare and contrast in a cooperative group is also good. The negative was that although the students were interested in the two vocalists, this type of nonfiction passage is unlikely to appear on their state assessment. A better choice would be a science or social studies passage that would support content vocabulary and concept learning and be closer to the kinds of passages that will appear on the assessment. Another alternative is to use the standards-based free high-interest passage to teach compare and contrast, then scaffold to the passage related to the standards-based curriculum and assessment.

PRACTICAL TIPS FOR HIGHER-LEVEL THINKING

All Content Areas in Grades 4–12

- Make a graphic organizer file that is accessible to students. Allow them to select one of the resources as needed to create a graphic representation of what they have read.
- Teach students a specific questioning strategy. Use it consistently.
- Use QAR. Make a QAR poster and have it in the room to prompt the teacher and support the students.
- Review by dividing the text into sections and assign each section to a group of 3–4 students. Each group should write one question for each of the QAR levels or levels of thinking. Students will ask their fellow students the questions as a review.
- Ask a trusted colleague to visit your classroom and provide feedback on the percentage of time you talk and the percentage of time you listen. The more you listen, the more students are doing the work and learning. Listen more, talk less.
- Reflect on the amount of time spent in class in which the teacher asks questions or tells students what she knows. Ask more questions, tell less. Set personal goals for asking more questions, and telling students less.
- Regardless of what is taught, show the joy of reading with nonfiction or fiction that includes content vocabulary and concepts. Here are some examples excellent for Grades 4–12. Each can be used to support content curriculum and joy in reading.

Mathematics:

Neuschwander, C. (1997). *Sir Cumference and the first round table: A math adventure.* Watertown, MA: Charlesbridge Publishers.
Sachar, L. (1994). *More sideways arithmetic from a wayside school.* New York: Scholastic, Inc.

Science:

Hiassen, C. (2002). *Hoot.* New York: Alfred A. Knopf.
Ryan, S. J. (2001). *Esmeralda and the enchanted pond.* Sarasota, FL: Pineapple Press.

Social Studies:

Murphy, J. (2003). *An American plague.* New York: Clarion Books.
Warren, A. (1996). *Orphan train rider: One boy's true story.* Boston: Houghton Mifflin.

English, Language Arts:

Ehrlich, A. (Ed). (2002). *When I was your age, volume two: Original stories about growing up.* Cambridge, MA: Candlewick Press.
Paulsen, G. (1999). *My life in dog years.* New York: Yearling Press.

- Prepare questions for the day's instruction in advance. Supplement textbook questions with higher-level questions.
- Do not accept general responses. Probe for specificity when students answer questions. "You said Hitler was a weak man. Can you tell me why you think that? Do you recall where you got that information—textbook, outside reading, television?"
- Use quickwrites to prepare students for the day's instruction, accessing prior knowledge or the previous day's work. Post the quickwrite on the board and have students begin writing as they take their seats. Call on students to share their quickwrites.
- Use 1-sentence summaries, evidence, and explain-your-answer techniques to improve writing and to assist students in showing their comprehension. "Write a 1-sentence summary of what you have learned in class today."

Engaging Parents and Community in Literacy Learning

Students whose parents are involved in the academic school experience tend to be good readers and are successful in school. Even for those who struggle and perhaps read below grade level, if their parents are involved in school, then parents provide a support system to ensure achievement. Consistent research suggests that parent and community involvement enhances student achievement (Henderson & Mapp, 2002) and is the basis for encouraging teachers, districts, and schools to include it in their fail-safe literacy systems. When follow-up monitoring takes place, it becomes clear that involving parents and community in literacy learning receives less attention than other components of the fail-safe literacy system. In a district of 35,000 that I have worked with to improve literacy, the literacy coaches and principals report that they want to engage parents and community, but it is the last task on the priority list. This is the reason why a chapter is included to remind you to substantively involve parents, families, and the community in literacy learning: We know that it will improve student achievement, but it is rarely implemented.

ENGAGING PARENTS

When students enter fourth grade, parents are beginning to be a little less involved than they were in the primary grades, particularly if their students are not experiencing success in school. As the students move through middle and high school, parental involvement decreases except for involvement in specific extracurricular activities like Band Boosters or

Athletic Boosters groups. Engaging parents in literacy learning does not refer to this type of involvement but rather to substantive involvement in literacy and academic experiences. These experiences may take place at home, at school, or in any other appropriate location.

Expectations for Literacy

It seems that the first issue to address is "Do parents want to be involved?" Yes! Parents want to be communicated with regarding academic expectations, grading procedures and practices, and opportunities to be engaged with their student's work.

To engage parents initially, provide multiple venues for knowledge of academic expectations. School and teacher Web sites provide opportunities to post assignments for the grading period, outside readings, projects, and, yes, even homework. In addition to assignments, expectations for grading should be posted or shared. This could take the form of a rubric, or grading scale. Sample work (without students' names, of course) could also be posted so the parents and students have models of excellent, mediocre, and unacceptable work.

With the availability of the Internet, plagiarism has skyrocketed. Take the opportunity to clarify what plagiarism means and what the consequences for plagiarism are. You may also want to refer them to a Web site that you will use for checking authenticity, such as www.turnitin.com.

In addition to technological venues for communication, printed information continues to be useful. With older students, you may want to mail materials home or ask for parent signatures if the communication is important. A historically low-performing middle school in Mobile, Alabama, worked tirelessly to improve student achievement and to engage parents, only to find that they had to budget for postage for mail communications to parents as the students did not take them home. Open-house nights and face-to-face meetings provide opportunities for direct interaction.

Engaging Parents in Assignments

Engaging parents substantively in their children's literacy learning will be rewarding for both. Think about how you can use the nonnegotiables to engage parents. Figure 7.1 provides you with a few ideas to consider. Please complete the figure with your own ideas on how you can substantively engage parents in literacy learning appropriate for your standards-based content. Think about sharing this template with parents so they know how you will teach, what you expect, and how they will be asked to support literacy learning at home. As a grade, team, or school,

Figure 7.1   Engaging Parents in Literacy Learning

Nonnegotiable Expectations of Daily Practice	Idea	Your Ideas
Print Rich	Ask parents to provide comments on student writing after being given the rubric. Post in the classroom. Ask parents to share their writing and post or contribute a favorite read to the classroom library.	
Literacy Processes	Ask students to preview a text with a family member. Ask students to interview a family member regarding a concept being studied and write down responses. Ask students to read to a parent. The parent will summarize what the student reads. Reverse the roles.	
Read To and With	Ask a family member to read a text with a student, with both completing a reflection. How do their reflections compare and contrast? Why do you suppose their reflections are different?	
Teach, Model, Practice Strategies	Provide parents with questions to ask the student after the student has read the text assigned. Questions should relate to prediction, connections, visualization, evaluation, or other comprehension strategies.	
Accountable Independent Reading	Once a week, expect students to read for 20 minutes at home and a family member to note that the student completed the task, after the accountability is written.	

you may decide that each teacher will format a template that is specific to his or her class and share with parents. This type of systematic effort pays off in improvements in student achievement.

Each of these ideas can be modified for the student to engage with any family member, either younger or older. Reading to a younger child enhances confidence and builds fluency, and is good literacy practice for both.

EDUCATING PARENTS IN LITERACY LEARNING

For those of us who have spent our careers teaching reading or assisting others to be successful with reading, writing, and content learning, helping our own children with schoolwork is natural. On the other hand, for noneducator parents, assisting their children may be difficult or even intimidating. Keep in mind that students who struggle with on-grade-level reading may have parents who had the same struggle and perhaps did not find the school experience to be engaging, rewarding, or enjoyable. On the other hand, parents who found school to be easy may not have the background to assist a struggling student. For parents for whom school was easy, it may be difficult to break their comprehension into the small chunks that can assist their students. These are reasons we do not want to assume that parents know what and how to assist with literacy learning. We want to honor parents with appropriate instruction.

Parent education should have the same components that the fail-safe classroom for literacy learning has. Teach, model, and practice with parents the nonnegotiables with respectful resources. With this understanding, they can support you at home. Teach them what questions to ask their students after school. When my son was in middle and high school, if I asked him how school was, he would answer, "Fine." He offered no additional information. Instead I learned that I had to ask him, "What did you read today?" or "What was particularly interesting out of all of your classes?" or "What surprised you today?"

Mental Model: Parent Literacy Learning

One middle school has a part-time parent liaison paid for from a grant. This parent liaison schedules monthly evening sessions with parents on a variety of topics. One of the monthly sessions was on literacy learning. As the speaker that evening, I had prepared a presentation on nonnegotiables and what parents could do to support those nonnegotiables at home. When the nonnegotiables were modeled, *Because of Winn-Dixie* by Kate DiCamillo and *Holes* by Louis Sachar were provided to each participant. Each parent received a copy of each text so everyone could participate. Most of the parents had their students with them in the audience. Pizza was served for dinner, and child care was provided for younger siblings so that the engagement would be high and distractions kept to a minimum.

The joy of reading was obvious as both the students and parents laughed, volunteered to read out loud, and volunteered to answer questions! They were particularly joyful when the evening concluded with the news that those who attended could take those books home and enjoy them with their entire family!

What made this evening particularly interesting is that the school is about 75% second-language learners, a high-poverty school, and one with many recent immigrants to the United States. The parents requested that the presentation be in Spanish, and the oral presentation and print materials were provided in both English and Spanish! This is an example of supporting parents where they are and engaging them in literacy learning, even if they are not fluent readers, writers, and speakers of English (Taylor & Gunter, 2005).

Mental Model: High School Family Literacy and Mathematics Night

A high school where I volunteer as a member of an oversight committee is working diligently to improve student achievement. The leadership knows that it must engage the parents and perhaps assist them with learning more about literacy. Recently the school held a Family Literacy and Mathematics Night. About 200 parents attended. This attendance represents about 20% of the student population, which is a huge turnout in this community. Teachers and school leaders shared what the students were learning related to literacy strategies and content. They also shared things parents could do at home. Last, parents were informed about the assessment that students must score proficiently on to receive a diploma.

Family Internet Resources

Complementary to direct opportunities for parents to learn expectations of literacy learning, teachers may want to check out the Web site for the publisher of the texts that the school regularly uses. Most publishers host parent windows on their Web sites.

Glencoe Publishers (www.glenco.com/sec/literature/parents) has a number of informative options for parents. There are supplementary reading lists for each text level and activities for parents to do with their students. www.Scholastic.com also has a family window with many options to engage parents of students up through middle school. Parents of high school students will also find this site helpful.

ENGAGING THE COMMUNITY

Library

There are many opportunities to engage the community in literacy learning. The most obvious one is to engage the free services of the local public library. Either take the students to the library or invite a library representative to the school to assist the students with obtaining a library card. Learning about the services available from the library will serve the students well. In addition to print materials, most libraries have Internet service for public use that students can use for research assignments. In our community, the library will mail books to the home for members so that they do not even have to make a special trip there.

In addition to the resources available, libraries have author events and celebrations related to literacy. Publicize these activities to your students and families, encouraging their participation. Annually, our community has an event called One Book, One Community. In recent years, the One Book has been *Esperanza Rising, Holes, Because of Winn-Dixie,* and *James and the Giant Peach.* During this time, the library in its various branches has related events, author visits, and celebrations to support the reading and discussion of the One Book for the community. The local newspaper participates with the One Book experience with ongoing activities, questions, writing contests for all ages, and a Web site for those reading and enjoying the book. Such a community reading and writing experience makes shared reading fun for the entire family and for students of all ages.

Service Organizations

Challenges that teachers continue to face include the development of a classroom library and the maintenance of appropriate supplementary resources, as was suggested in Chapter 6. Think about making a literacy presentation to service organizations like the Junior League, Lions Club, or Rotary, offering suggestions for service projects. They could adopt a class and assist with collecting appropriate paperback books for the classroom collection or sponsor appropriate classroom magazine subscriptions for the class or for individual students who cannot afford them.

For-Profit Companies

One of the hottest commodities these days is books. Bookstores and coffee shops do a great deal of business and provide literary events for the community. Watch for author signings and events related to texts that are appropriate for and of interest to your students. Develop a professional relationship with the local manager and ask him how he would like to get involved with your literacy efforts. In return, offer to support his marketing needs.

When thinking about for-profit companies, remember your book clubs and book fairs. The parents who tend to participate probably already have students who read well. Sebastian River High School is committed to improving literacy for all of its students. It moved the book fair to the migrant community from which it draws its most challenged students. This significant effort was to inform parents, provide opportunity, and make a huge statement related to supporting literacy learning.

Mental Model: Community Engagement

An exemplary community engagement example takes place in my local high school, Timber Creek. Timber Creek has partnered with Barney's Coffee to develop the Beans and Books Café. As you enter the school's library, to the left you see a room with striped awnings on the windows and bistro tables outside. As you enter Beans and Books Café, you find a small Barney's Coffee bar, more bistro tables, and kiosks full of books. Students and faculty are browsing books, sitting at bistro tables reading, and enjoying refreshments. This is an exemplary example of respecting the developmental stage of students, connecting it to their world, and providing joy in reading!

VOLUNTEERS

One of the most common and obvious ways to engage the community in literacy learning is to engage service organizations, retirees, college students, and other community-minded individuals in tutoring both during and after school. Wanting to be helpful is important but not sufficient for enhancing literacy learning. After a successful background check and before any volunteer is allowed to tutor any student of any age, you are encouraged to provide literacy learning education for volunteers. Teach them the nonnegotiables, give them specific tasks to accomplish, and monitor the success carefully.

An example of a successful volunteerism literacy project takes place in Marietta, Georgia. The project is called RISE. RISE is coordinated by the school visiting teacher and social worker. She accepts applications for RISE from high school seniors to tutor in the feeder elementary school. Those accepted receive specific instruction in guided reading, develop instructional plans for the students they tutor, and are monitored for their work. Students who receive this tutoring have more than a year's measurable growth in reading. At the end of the school year, the elementary students, tutors, teachers, and families have a celebration of reading and learning, where recognition is awarded along with a specially selected book that is just right for the young reader.

Although these are high school students receiving credit for tutoring elementary students, the same model can be applied to any tutor working at any grade level. The key components are education, clear expectations, and monitoring (Taylor & Peterson, 2003).

SERVICE LEARNING

Conway Middle School, as part of a service learning project, had students write short books with illustrations and make a lap quilt to accompany the book. Each of the books and lap quilts was given to a terminally ill child. Prior to these books being given to the children, they were shared with the public at Barnes and Noble's "open-mike night." At this event, students read their books to the audience and received feedback and applause. This service learning project included all of the processes of literacy.

Mental Model: Literacy in Service Learning

There is a wonderful book, *Sitti's Secrets*, by Naomi Shibab Nye. The book is about a young girl who goes to the other side of the world to visit her *sitti*, or grandma. They do not speak the same language, but they find ways to communicate and develop a special relationship. Her sitti has a box with remembrances of days past that she does not want to forget. It securely holds a piece of thread, velvet of a special dress, photos, and other concrete objects that conjure up beautiful memories.

Nancy, a curriculum resource teacher, read this adolescent picture book to a special-needs class. When she had completed the reading and the discussion, she told the students she was thinking about the assisted-living center near the school. "Did this book give you any ideas related to the assisted-living center?" Nancy asked the students. Well, it certainly did. The students decided that they would gather examples of concrete objects, like balls, ribbon, or pictures, and make a memory box to take on a visit to the assisted-living center. On their visits, they invited the residents to select an object from the memory box and share with students their memories or oral history. Students wrote the oral history as it was conveyed to them.

Before going to the assisted-living center, the students introduced themselves by way of the Internet with their self-descriptions and photos. This is an exemplary example of a service learning project using literacy and literacy processes to develop historical perspectives, contribute to the community, and improve reading and writing.

REFLECTION ON IMPROVING
READING, WRITING, AND CONTENT LEARNING

The fail-safe literacy point of view when consistently practiced in classrooms results in higher student achievement. This means that the nonnegotiable expectations of daily practice are present. These practices provide access to on-grade-level content while at the same time developing independent readers, writers, and content learners.

Furthermore, for students to perform better on the reading-comprehension section of standardized assessment, align the daily classroom experience with the assessment. This means that the students should read nonfiction at least in the proportion they are expected to read nonfiction on the assessment. Ask questions at all levels daily, using respectful, aligned materials that assist you in scaffolding students to higher levels of thinking and achievement on reading comprehension on standardized assessments. Require students to write short responses in complete sentences, then scaffold to longer writing samples by combining shorter pieces.

To assist the reader with self-reflection on these concepts, a Teacher Reflection Guide is provided in the Resources. I encourage the reader to periodically review the Teacher Reflection Guide to remind yourself of the research-based practices that you are using and to celebrate your successes!

PRACTICAL TIPS FOR ENGAGING PARENTS
AND COMMUNITY IN LITERACY LEARNING

- Develop a positive relationship with parents and community by inviting them to participate.
- Educate parents and community on student expectations for improving reading, writing, and content learning.
- Educate the community on what is needed: subscriptions, books, volunteers, tutors, etc.
- Provide explicit instruction and expectations in reading and writing for tutors and volunteers.
- Utilize literacy in service learning projects.
- Go to the parents and community (churches, Boys and Girls Clubs, service organizations, etc.); do not expect them to come to you.

Resource A: Teacher Reflection Guide

Teacher Reflection Guide

Part 1. Reading Components

1. What did students do to develop vocabulary today?

2. What did students do to improve fluency?

3. How did students strategize to comprehend the text?

4. What will I do differently next time?

Part 2. Framing Print Instruction With Before-, During-, and After-Reading Strategies

1. What strategies did I use today?

   Before reading

   During reading

   After reading

2. Which ones worked really well?

   Before reading

   During reading

   After reading

3. What will I try next time?

   Before reading

   During reading

   After reading

Part 3. High Levels of Thinking

1. What levels of thinking did students work on today?

2. Which questions were at levels of analysis, synthesis, and evaluation?

3. Which levels of thinking will students work on tomorrow?

4. Who developed the questions today—teacher or students?

Part 4. Questioning

1. What questioning strategies did I use today?

2. Which questioning strategies worked well?

3. Which ones will I work on tomorrow?

4. Did I call on every student?

5. Did I validate every student?

6. Were incorrect responses corrected and confirmed, clarifying meaning?

7. Were questions asked on all levels, low to high?

Part 5. Writing

1. How was writing used to develop vocabulary?

2. How was writing used for students to show comprehension?

3. How was writing used before, during, and after reading?

4. Did students write down their questions before we answered them?

5. Did students peer-review writing and provide feedback?

6. Do students have the rubric for grading? Is it always consistent?

Resource B: Accountable Independent Reading Log

Accountable Independent Reading Log

Student: _____ Book: _____ Author: _____ Genre: _____

Date	Ending page, paragraph	Visualization, connection, 1-sentence summary, prediction, or evaluation	Interesting words/page

Resource C:
Book Talk Checklist

Book Talk Checklist

Student: _____ Book: _____ Author: _____ Genre: _____

Directions: Please assign up to 5 points for each of the five categories on the checklist. Sign your name after totaling up the points you are awarding the student. Each student will give the book talk 4 times, one time to each of 4 different adults, earning a possible total of 100 points.

Category	Listener 1	Listener 2	Listener 3	Listener 4
Title is explained (5)				
Plot or main points are discussed (5)				
Speaking: tone, pronunciation, grammar, enthusiasm (5)				
Persuades the listener to read the book (5)				
Overall quality of the book talk (5)				
Total:				
Signature:				
Comments:				

Note: This book talk checklist was designed for students who are giving book talks to adults in the school and receiving feedback. It may also be used for book talks to individual students or to the class.

References

Action Magazine. New York: Scholastic, Inc.

Allen, J. (2004). *Tools for teaching content literacy.* Portland, ME: Stenhouse Publishers.

Allen, J., & Daley, P. (2004). *Read-aloud anthology.* New York: Scholastic, Inc.

Barton, M. L., & Heidman, C. (2002). *Teaching reading in mathematics* (2nd ed.). Aurora, CO: McREL.

Barton, M. L., & Jordan, D. L. (2001). *Teaching reading in science.* Aurora, CO: McREL.

Beers, K. (2003). *When kids can't read: What teachers can do.* Portsmouth, NH: Heinemann.

Bellamo, T. S. (2005*). Latinate word parts and vocabulary: Contrasts among three groups comprising community college preparatory reading class.* Unpublished doctoral dissertation. University of Central Florida, Orlando.

Biancarosa, G., & Snow, C. (2004). *Reading next: A vision for action and research in middle and high school literacy.* New York: Carnegie Corporation.

Billmeyer, R., & Barton, M. L. (1998). *Teaching reading in the content areas: If not me, then who?* Aurora, CO: McREL.

Bloom, B. S., Englehart, M. D., Farst, E. J., Hill, W. H., & Krathwohl, D. R. (1956). *A taxonomy of educational objectives: Handbook I, the cognitive domain.* New York: David McKay Co.

Bluford series. (2004). West Berlin, NJ: Townsend Press.

Burmark, H. L. (2004). *Visual literacy: Learn to see, see to learn.* Alexandria, VA: ASCD.

Cisneros, S. (1984). *The house on Mango Street.* New York: Vintage Books.

Cognition and Technology Group at Vanderbilt. (1990). Anchored instruction and its relationship to situated cognition. *Educational Researcher, 19*(6), 2–10.

Coney, F. (1996). *Orange County literacy project evaluation.* Orlando, FL: Orange County Public Schools. Unpublished report.

Dahl, R. (1961). *James and the giant peach.* New York: Alfred Knopf Inc.

Daniels, H., & Zimmerman, S. (2004). *Subjects matter.* Portsmouth, NH: Heinemann.

DiCamillo, K. (2000). *Because of Winn-Dixie.* Cambridge, MA: Candlewick Press.

Ehrlich, A. (Ed) (2002). *When I was your age, volume two: Original stories about growing up.* Cambridge, MA: Candlewick Press.

Feldman, K., & Kinsella, K. (2004). *Narrowing the language gap: The case for explicit vocabulary instruction.* New York: Scholastic.

Fleischman, P. (1988). *Joyful noise: Poems for two voices.* New York: Harper Trophy.

Fleischman, P. (1997). *Seedfolks.* New York: Harper Trophy.

Good, T. L. (1982). How teachers' expectations affect results. *American Education, 18*(10), 25–32.

Good, T. L. & Brophy, J. E. (1994). *Looking in classrooms* (6th ed.). New York: HarperCollins.

Graves, M., & Fitzgerald, J. (2002). Scaffolding reading experiences for multilingual classrooms. In G. Garcia (Ed.), *English learners: Reaching the highest level of English literacy* (pp. 96–124). Newark, DE: International Reading Association.

Helping struggling readers at the elementary and secondary school levels. (2002). Arlington, VA: Educational Research Service.

Henderson, A. T., & Mapp, K. L. (2002). *A new wave of evidence: The impact of school, family, & community connections and student achievement.* Austin, TX: National Center for Family & Community Connections With Schools.

Hiassen, C. (2002). *Hoot.* New York: Alfred A. Knopf.

Irvin, J. (1998). *Reading and the middle school student: Strategies to enhance literacy.* Boston: Allyn & Bacon.

Jackson, P. (1995). *Sacred hoops.* New York: Hyperion.

Jensen, E. (1998). *Teaching with the brain in mind.* Alexandria, VA: ASCD.

Krull, K. (1996). *Wilma unlimited: How Wilma Rudolph became the fastest woman in the world.* San Diego, CA: Voyager Books.

Kulling, M. (2000). *Escape north: The story of Harriet Tubman.* New York: Random House.

Langer, J. A. (2000). *Achieving high-quality reading and writing in an urban middle school: The case of Gail Slatko.* The National Center for English Language Learning & Achievement. [On-line]. Available at http://cela.albany.edu

Marzano, R. J. (2004). *Building background knowledge for academic achievement.* Alexandria, VA: ASCD.

Marzano, R. J., Pickering, D. J., & Pollock, J. E. (2001). *Classroom instruction that works: Research-based strategies for increasing student achievement.* Alexandria, VA: ASCD.

Munoz-Ryan, P. (2000). *Esperanza rising.* New York: Scholastic, Inc.

Murphy, J. (2003). *An American plague.* New York: Clarion Books.

National Institute of Child Health and Human Development. (2000). *Report of the national reading panel. Teaching children to read. An evidence-based assessment of scientific research literature on reading and implications for reading instruction.* Bethesda, MD: U.S. Department of Health and Human Services.

Nation's Report Card. (2005). Retrieved March 3, 2006, from www.nationsreport card.gov

Neuschwander, C. (1997). *Sir Cumference and the first Round Table: A math adventure.* Watertown, MA: Charlesbridge Publishing.

North Central Regional Education Laboratory (NCREL). (2004, May 12). *A closer look at the five essential components of effective reading instruction: A review of scientifically based reading research for teachers.* Retrieved April 14, 2005, from http://www.ncrel.org/rf/components.pdf

Nye, N. S. (1997). *Sitti's secrets.* New York: Aladdin Paperbacks.

Paulsen, G. (1999). *My life in dog years.* New York: Yearling Press.

Pinnell, G., Pikulski, J., Wixson, K., Campbell, J., Gough, P., & Beatty, A. (1995). *Listening to children read aloud.* Washington, DC: Office of Educational Research and Improvement, U.S. Department of Education.

Rasinski, T. V. (2003). *The fluent reader: Oral reading strategies for building word recognition, fluency, and comprehension.* New York: Scholastic, Inc.

Read XL. (1999). New York: Scholastic, Inc.

Robb, L. (2000). *Teaching reading in middle school.* New York: Scholastic, Inc.

Robb, L. (2002). *Reader's handbook.* Wilmington, MA: Great Source.

Rowe, M. B. (1986, January–February). Wait time: Slowing down may be a way of speeding up. *The Journal of Teacher Education, 31*(1), 43–50.

Ryan, S. J. (2001). *Esmeralda and the enchanted pond.* Sarasota, FL: Pineapple Press.

Sachar, L. (1994). *More sideways arithmetic from a wayside school.* New York: Scholastic, Inc.

Sachar, L. (1998). *Holes.* New York: Yearling Books.

Science World. New York: Scholastic, Inc.

Scope Magazine. New York: Scholastic, Inc.

Sourcebook. (2004). Wilmington, MA: Great Source.

Spring Board. (2004). Princeton, NJ: College Board.

Stallings, J. (1980). Allocated academic learning time revisited, or beyond time on task. *Educational Researcher, 8*(11), 11–16.

Stephens, E. C., & Brown, J. E. (2000). *A handbook of content literacy strategies: 75 practical reading and writing ideas.* Norwood, MA: Christopher-Gordon Publishers.

Taylor, R., & Collins, V. D. (2003). *Literacy leadership for grades 5–12.* Alexandria, VA: ASCD.

Taylor, R. T., & Gunter, G. A. (2005). *The K–12 literacy leadership fieldbook.* Thousand Oaks, CA: Corwin Press.

Taylor, R. T., & Peterson, D. S. (2003, Winter). RISE: Service and learning combine. *Kappa Delta Phi Record, 39*(2), 70–73.

Time for Kids. Boston: Houghton Mifflin.

Tomlinson, C., & Kalbfleisch, M. (1998). Teach me, teach my brain: A call for differentiated classrooms. *Educational Leadership, 3*(56), 52–55.

Trelease, J. (2001). *The read aloud handbook* (5th ed.). New York: Penguin Books.

Upfront. New York: Scholastic, Inc.

Warren, A. (1996). *Orphan train rider: One boy's true story.* Boston: Houghton Mifflin.

Webb, N. L. (1999). *Alignment between standards & assessment.* Madison, WI: University of Wisconsin Center for Educational Research.

Wilson, E. A. (2004). *READING at the middle and high school levels: Building active readers across the curriculum* (3rd ed.). Arlington, VA: Educational Research Service.

Zutell, J., & Rasinski, T. (1991). Training teachers to attend to their students' oral reading fluency. *Theory Into Practice, 30,* 211–217.

Index

CORWIN PRESS

The Corwin Press logo—a raven striding across an open book—represents the union of courage and learning. Corwin Press is committed to improving education for all learners by publishing books and other professional development resources for those serving the field of PreK–12 education. By providing practical, hands-on materials, Corwin Press continues to carry out the promise of its motto: **"Helping Educators Do Their Work Better."**